Seeing God Through Science

Seeing God Through Science

Exploring the Science Narrative to Strengthen
and Deepen Faith in the Creator

Barry David Schoub

WIPF & STOCK · Eugene, Oregon

SEEING GOD THROUGH SCIENCE
Exploring the Science Narrative to Strengthen and Deepen Faith in the Creator

Copyright © 2019 Barry David Schoub. All rights reserved. Except for brief quotations in critical publications or reviews, no part of this book may be reproduced in any manner without prior written permission from the publisher. Write: Permissions, Wipf and Stock Publishers, 199 W. 8th Ave., Suite 3, Eugene, OR 97401.

Wipf & Stock
An Imprint of Wipf and Stock Publishers
199 W. 8th Ave., Suite 3
Eugene, OR 97401

www.wipfandstock.com

PAPERBACK ISBN: 978-1-5326-8712-9
HARDCOVER ISBN: 978-1-5326-8713-6
EBOOK ISBN: 978-1-5326-8714-3

All scriptural quotations are taken from the JPS Hebrew-English *Tanakh*, with kind permission of the Jewish Publication Society.

Manufactured in the U.S.A.

With deepest gratitude to my Creator.

This book is dedicated in great affection to my dear wife Barbara on the occasion of our golden wedding anniversary, and to our dear children, Wendy, Richard, and Peter, and their families.

Contents

Preface | ix
Acknowledgments | xiii

Introduction | 1
1. The Search for Truth | 11
2. Science and Meta-Science | 24
3. Design and Frontiers | 44
4. The Human Organism and the Human Soul | 66
5. Non-Predicate Theism | 79
6. Divine Revelation | 94
7. Addressing Atheism, Theism and Science | 106
8. Epilogue | 125

Bibliography | 139
Author Index | 151
Subject Index | 153
Scripture Index | 163

List of Tables

Table 1. The Flow of Scientific Investigation | 26
Table 2. The Scientific Process vs the Religious Process | 28

Preface

I HAVE FOR SEVERAL years contemplated writing a book on my personal approach to the oft contentious subject of science and religion. I am neither a professional theologian nor am I a professional philosopher. What has motivated me to put pen to paper is a more than four-decade career that I have enjoyed as a professional biomedical scientist, as well as savoring a deeply meaningful life as a practicing member of the Orthodox Jewish faith. As Lord Bertrand Russell famously said: "Science is what you know. Philosophy is what you don't know." Perhaps, then, it is my background in science (that, I guess I do know), which might sanction my foray into the uncertain sphere of the philosophy of religion—uncertain because there appears to be no general clarity on what "philosophy" or "religion" truly mean. Certainly, it is very clear to us scientists what science means, and what it defines and explains. However, pleas have been made, an example of which I have mentioned in the introductory chapter, for science to look to philosophy to broaden itself beyond its hard, cold facts. More than that, I have felt that science also needs to broaden itself into the realm of theology.

Synchronizing religion with science is becoming relatively uncommon in the modern hyper-secular society and even rarer in the academic scientific community (more usually it is the asynchrony of science *or* religion). In the many years that I have participated in scientific meetings, rubbing shoulders with my colleagues from around the globe, religion and science would, on not a few occasions, become a topic for tea-time discussion, as my Orthodox Jewish dietary requirements, and my avoidance of work or travel on Saturdays, declared my religious observance. I have, indeed, found it sad that science and scientific knowledge form the paramount tool for non-belief. The statistic which I quote in the introductory chapter of the book of only 7 percent of members of the National Academy of Sciences of the United States believing in a deity, reflected the similar experience I encountered with my own scientific colleagues. I remain, nevertheless, a fervent science patriot. It is indeed difficult not to be overawed with the achievements that twenty-first-century science has made to advance our understanding of the universe, as well as to vastly improve the quality of life of humankind.

It is certainly true that eminent scientists such as Francis Collins (*The Language of God*, Free Press, 2006) and John Polkinghorne (*Science and Religion in Quest of Truth*, Yale University Press, 2011), and theologians such as Jonathan Sacks (*The Great Partnership*, Schocken, 2012), have produced books of great value, substantiating a highly successful symbiotic relationship between science and religion. So why yet another publication on this subject? What ideas can be added to these publications, as well as to the many debates and discussions on the subject, much of which is widely available to the public on the internet? I aim to demonstrate in this book a somewhat different nuance to the more directed approach which these other authors have taken regarding the symbiotic relationship between science and religion. Firstly, I have focused much of my discussion directly on what science reveals, i.e., the science used by atheists to support their claims for the non-existence of God. Nevertheless, it is this science which contributes to the very evidence to support belief in God. The staggering integrated complexity and the overwhelming beauty of the universe, which science reveals, and which continues to be revealed with ever-increasing grandeur, compellingly generates the questions of meaning and purpose. However, meaning and purpose are questions which atheists prefer to avoid; and yet, it is these very questions which thinking humans seek to have answered.

There is a further important feature of the scientific enterprise which I will elaborate on in the book—that of meta-science, i.e.

the characteristic pattern of the unfolding of scientific knowledge. This very distinctive pattern repeats itself over and over again with each scientific "breakthrough," and in every scientific discipline. Each onward step is followed by the further forward shift of the knowledge frontier. This Sisyphean disposition of science, which I will elaborate on in the book, runs counter to the hubris of the materialist, scientism-oriented non-believer, that science will eventually answer all reality and, therefore, there is no need to resort to any supernatural belief. There is, however, a consideration which needs to be borne in mind in relation to any exclusive admiration of science—that science is a human construct, and the history of scientific achievement reflects what the limits are to what it can reveal. By definition, science operates only within the universe of natural phenomena and, even within natural phenomena, meta-science seems to indicate that there also is, and will continue to be, a limit to the extent of scientific discovery, even within the natural world. It is therefore inapplicable to utilize scientific agencies to explore and investigate the supernatural being.

Manipulations of language and anthropomorphic fallacies are often favored ploys used by atheists to discredit religious faith, but humans are not able to assign attributes to God. Anthropomorphic allusions in the Bible and omni- (omnipotent, omniscient, and omni-benevolent) references to God, serve only to utilize human language to make what God communicates to humankind, understandable. They do not qualify any Divine attribute. I have formulated the term "non-predicate theism" to affirm this cardinal concept. This idea is analogous to the apophatic theology of the early Christian religion and the negative theology of Maimonides in the Jewish religion, but it has now regained its importance in the modern scientific era.

It behooves me to request two indulgences from my readers of this book. Firstly, there is some degree of what is unavoidable gender insensitivity. I tried as far as possible to use the gender-neutral terms of "human" or "humankind." However, in some cases, especially when referring to biblical texts, I have followed the convention of

PREFACE

using the male pronoun for references to God and, of course, in quotations, I have remained faithful to the original words used. Secondly, as mentioned above, I am of the Orthodox Jewish faith, and much of the text is oriented to this religion. However I do hope that non-Jewish religious readers would be able to transpose these ideas appropriately into their respective faiths.

Barry D Schoub
Johannesburg, South Africa
2019

Acknowledgments

My sincere thanks to my wife Barbara for proofreading the manuscript and valuable suggestions.

Introduction

A knowledge of the historic and philosophical background gives that kind of independence from prejudices of his generation from which most scientists are suffering. This independence created by philosophical insight is—in my opinion—the mark of distinction between a mere artisan or specialist and a real seeker after truth.

—ALBERT EINSTEIN, LETTER TO ROBERT THORNTON

IN AN ARTICLE PUBLISHED recently in the Proceedings of the National Academy of Sciences of the USA entitled "Why Science Needs Philosophy," Laplane and colleagues make a plea for establishing and promoting communication between philosophers and scientists.[1] The increasing specialization of the science of today stands in danger of losing its constituent of the deep reflection which it needs to innovate concepts and visionary ideas. The person of the scientist-philosopher who, in the past, melded the two domains of thought, may now be receding into history, to the detriment of modern science. The pressure to publish and to produce data is in danger of fashioning many scientists into technologists, engineers, and artisans, rather than seekers of knowledge who probe, innovate, and reflect on the information that science research provides. The pressure to produce data, which is so characteristic of the modern scientific enterprise, compromises the ability to look beyond

---

1. Laplane et al., "Why Science Needs Philosophy," 3948–52.

the material. Entering into the science-religion debate, defenders of non-belief have a propensity to restrict intellectual probing to within the physical realm only. The constructs of philosophy are undoubtedly of great value in broadening the capability of the scientific method, and dialogue between philosophers and scientists is undoubtedly mutually beneficial.[2] As science would benefit from philosophy, and philosophy benefit from science, so would theology benefit from science and, I would venture to propose, the reverse would also be of great value. Regrettably, in the modern era as great a rift as there is between philosophy and science, there is an even greater schism between science and theology. There is little doubt that the physical focus of modern science makes the concept of theism even more in need of defense.

Why defend theism? Should theism be defended merely because of the knock-on benefits to human society? However, in the religion-atheism debate, there is little that is more contentious than this point of dispute. Atheists will be very quick to point out that throughout the history of humankind, most blood has been spilled in religious wars. Furthermore, in more recent times, the weaponization of religion has graphically exemplified the depravity of religious violence when used to serve political goals through terrorism. (On the other hand, it could be pointed out that the most horrific genocidal conflicts of the twentieth century, under Stalin, Hitler, and Pol Pot, were not driven by religion.) There can be no doubt that the concoction of religion and politics produces an incendiary mixture.[3]

Does religion benefit society? The costs of society's ills in the affluent developed world which are due to the rejection of religion, and which has accompanied modernization and secularization, has been well documented.[4] The psychological benefits of religion to the individual, and the sociological benefits of religion to society, will undoubtedly engender its own debate between believers and nonbelievers. (Epidemiological studies demonstrating a

2. Laplane et al., *Science Needs Philosophy*, 3948–52.
3 See Sacks, *Not in God's Name*, esp. 231–37.
4. Galtung, "On the Social Costs," 379–413.

significantly reduced mortality in religiously observant communities may, perhaps, be more relevant to today's self-interested pragmatic individual.)[5] However, these considerations do lie outside the ambit of this volume and will not be discussed further. The scope of this book will focus on investigating the essential truth statement of religious belief, which is basically divisible into three components:

1. Does God exist?
2. Did God create the world?
3. Does God control and govern the world?

Pondering on the complexity, the beauty, and the synchrony of the world we live in, we seek answers to where all of what we see and experience came from. Why does this all exist? And what does all of this mean? To many thinkers, modern science may well provide the complete answers to satisfy these inquiries. Why there are droughts, earthquakes, and plagues is now largely understandable; how matter is constituted, what lies beyond the Milky Way, and even how the human species came about, are all becoming more transparent with the enormous progress of the modern scientific enterprise. At the same time, the creed of scientific humanism (or secular humanism) is being offered to serve as an alternate to religion. Science and humanism are dispensing with the need to search for the existence of God, and instead purport to utilize human reason for logical inquiry, and ethical norms for structuring society. All of this is based on a naturalistic explanation of the world, and reality as defined through scientific knowledge.

This book will posit a contrary interpretation of science. It will aim to demonstrate that science and religion are far from being in conflict with each other. Indeed, it is the very science narrative itself, which is a divine gift to humankind, and which furnishes humans with the fundamental evidence for the existence of the Creator—who lies outside the naturalistic world he created. What science has achieved is to develop the framework of those

---

5. Kim and VanderWeele, "Mediators," 96–101.

questions that plead for a meaningful response to those inquiries which lie beyond nature. These are the questions of the origin, the meaning, the purpose, and the governance of a universe revealed by science. In addition to details of the grandeur and the complexity of the universe unveiled to humankind by science, it is also the very process of scientific exploration itself, i.e., meta-science, which generates its own questions. The answers to these questions provide further compelling support for belief in a reality that lies beyond the naturalistic world of science.

It is clear that religion in the developed world, which is inadequately supported by an intellectual foundation, is becoming progressively more vulnerable to non-belief, largely proportional to the veritable explosion of modern scientific knowledge. The question has even been asked whether religion can survive the inexorable march of science.[6] There are, in fact, some claims that the fastest growing "religion" in the West, particularly in Western Europe, is "no religion." In a recent Pew Research Center survey, the religiously unaffiliated — referred to as the "nones"—accounted for 16 percent of the world's population.[7] In the Americas and Europe the "nones" constituted the second largest religious group, making up a quarter or more of the population. In the United Kingdom and Germany a *National Geographic* study predicted "that religion would fade from relevancy as the world modernizes" and countries such as France, Netherlands, New Zealand, United Kingdom and Australia "will soon have majority secular populations."[8] The manifest progress of atheism is best illustrated by studies of the religious affiliation in the youth. A study commissioned by the Benedict XVI Center for Religion and Society, published in 2018, found that 70 percent of young adults (aged 16 to 29) in the United Kingdom, 64 percent in France, 75 percent in Sweden, and as high as 91 percent in the Czech Republic, professed to having no religious affiliation ("nones").[9] The former

6. "Is God Dead?"
7. Pew Research Center, "Second Largest Religious Group."
8. Bullard, "World's Newest Major Religion."
9. Bullivant, "Europe's Young Adults and Religion," 1–11.

INTRODUCTION

Archbishop of Canterbury, Lord Carey, in an article in the Telegraph of London, warned that Christianity could be a generation away from extinction in Britain.[10]

Much of the so-called "crisis of faith" is attributable to the burgeoning of scientific knowledge over the last several decades. Unsurprisingly, in the scientific community itself, only one-third of scientists belonging to the American Association for the Advancement of Science (AAAS) believe in God.[11] A poll of the elite United States National Academy of Science found that from a low of only 5.5 percent of biological scientists to a high of 14.3 percent of mathematicians believe in a personal God.[12] Scientism and various related secular ideologies, which are disseminated widely through the pervasive electronic media, are progressively replacing religion in current thought and belief. In the modern mechanistic world, truth is coming to be defined by scientific progress, and morality by secular artifactual humanism. Human reasoning and philosophical reflection, which previously sought answers to reality, and probed deeply beyond the cognitive experience, have now, to a large extent, been replaced by scientific algorithmic reasoning. And so in the scientific world the ontological questions remain unanswered, and enquiry into what constitutes ultimate reality is usually simply avoided.

Reflections on the relationship between science and religion and, in particular, that science could eventually replace the need for religion, go back almost as far as the written history of humankind. Already over two millennia ago, the legendary father of medicine, Hippocrates (460–370 BCE) pondered on the God of the gaps issue—that science will ultimately explain those aspects of reality which are currently unexplained:

> People think that epilepsy is divine simply because they don't have an idea what causes epilepsy. But I believe that someday we will understand what causes epilepsy, and

10. Bingham, "Christianity at Risk."
11. Larson and Witham, "Leading Scientists," 313.
12. Brooks and Phillips, "Beyond Belief," 8–11.

at that moment, we will cease to believe that it is divine. And so it is with everything in the universe.[13]

Are the paths that science and religion seek for truth, in fact, antagonistic? Are they doctrines that compete with each other and are irreconcilable? The science-religion debate has, for centuries, spawned positions ranging from opposition, ideological separation, accommodation, incorporation, to symbiotic partnership.

Firstly, there is the atheist view, which simply rejects the existence of God and which, in the modern era, largely rests on the foundation that science refutes religion. As Jerry Coyne has put it:

> Science and religion aren't friends . . . Science and faith are fundamentally incompatible and for precisely the same reason that irrationality and rationality are incompatible . . . Their ways of understanding the universe are irreconcilable.[14]

A second approach to accommodate both science and religion is that of Stephen Jay Gould's "non-overlapping magisteria" (NOMA), which dissociates science from religion and compartmentalizes them into independent non-overlapping areas of inquiry —science analyzing physical phenomena, while religion concerns itself with values, ethics, and morality.[15] Most theists, as well as non-believers, do not hold with this view.[16] Both science and religion are human efforts to search for truth, and they clearly do overlap, not only in their goals of enquiry, but very much so in the intersecting grey areas of their investigations, analyses, and interpretations.

A third approach to the science and religion dialogue is complementarity, symbiosis, and mutual support. In recent times this has been reflected in the number of publications that accommodate, recognize, and value scientific knowledge within the sphere

---

13. Desai and Sadrieh, "It's Time to Remember Hippocrates," 501–2.
14. Coyne, "Science and Religion Aren't Friends," 10A.
15. Gardner, "Religious Views," 8–13.
16. Rational Wiki, "Non-Overlapping Magisteria."

of religious belief,[17] including the proposition of a partnership between science and religion.[18] This standpoint does need, in my view, further elaboration and qualification. Science is, of course, a human creation—a sensory, cognitive, and analytical activity to understand the mechanics of the universe; but it is, nevertheless, still a human activity. The creation of the universe, from a theistic viewpoint, was a supernatural event and as a consequence the elements and the essence of the creator are, *ipso facto*, beyond natural human cognitive competency. They lie beyond scientific investigation and beyond the realm of scientific evidence. As remarkable and even awe-inspiring as science reveals the created universe to be, scientific revelations of the elements of the universe cannot in themselves provide evidence of the existence of the creator of that universe. As I mentioned above, my proposition is that the role of the bountiful products of the scientific industry is to formulate the consequential questions that arise from these endeavors. It is these questions which constitute the initial components of what then becomes evidence-based theism. However, I fear that there is a potential difficulty in defending religious belief primarily through citing selected scientific findings, and even more so by employing the varieties of the "God of the gaps" arguments.[19] These arguments precariously render the case for God vulnerable to the dynamic changes which are so part and parcel of science-based knowledge—this will be discussed further in chapter 2, see pgs. 32–33.

I am, in addition, also proposing in this book, another theistic idea of science's contribution to religious belief. I am suggesting that, beyond simply addressing the content of science in isolation, as important and relevant as it is, one also needs to take into account the process by which scientific knowledge advances, i.e., meta-science. This process is characterized by a perpetually expanding frontier of the unknown—a constantly advancing frontier of knowledge and a receding horizon of non-knowledge

17. Collins, *Language of God*; Miller, *Finding Darwin's God*; Polkinghorne, *Science and Religion*.

18. Sacks, *Great Partnership*.

19. See Pennock, "Argument from Ignorance," 309–38.

beyond the reach of human beings. The characteristics of this process communicates a message of a reality which lies beyond the scientifically demonstrable, a reality which, consequently, testifies to the existence of a supernatural creator. In other words, meta-science teaches humankind that it does not possess the capability of fully understanding the universe, and it declares a reality that is beyond human comprehension. The recognition and appreciation of this reality conveys a message and furnishes evidence of a being beyond natural knowledge—the supernatural creator and controller of the universe, God.

On my journey through science and religion, I have come to recognize that the meta-science process is Sisyphean[20] in nature—research and investigation answering the questions of science which, in turn, beget even more questions resulting from the answers to the original questions. Viewed in its totality, scientific progress seems to be characterized by the never-ending frontiers to knowledge—seemingly indicating that the goal of comprehensive total knowledge is unreachable to human enquiry. Despite the hubris of claims by scientists, especially non-believing scientists, that eventually science will elucidate every extant enigma, the history of scientific discovery clearly does not bear this out. Even when it may appear that only a few "loose ends" remain, solving those "loose ends" often simply generates far more "loose ends" to be investigated. The knowledge treadmill and the retreating horizon of a universe beyond the reach of human science is deserving of deeper reflection as to what it signifies. A meaningful explanation of that reality which lies beyond science cannot come from science. It comes through revelation from the personal God.

I believe that no serious scientist doubts the authenticity and the validity of the scientific enterprise in providing our vast knowledge of the workings of the universe, and no intellectually honest theist can seriously challenge the truth value of science. The non-scientist may not be familiar with the rigor

---

20. The mythical king Sisyphus, was punished by the gods for the sins of self-aggrandizement and deceit and condemned to perpetually roll a boulder up the hill, only for it to roll down again as he neared the summit.

INTRODUCTION

and the extent to which verification tools are built into the scientific method to ensure the validity and authenticity of scientific knowledge. For this reason I have detailed in some length the process of scientific investigation in chapter 2, see pgs. 26–29. What has struck me, as an observer and participant in decades of unfolding science, is that there is a profound religious message reflected in the motif of scientific progress, as I have outlined. In other words the progress of science, as spectacular as it has been, and as remarkable as the technological spin-offs have benefitted humankind, teaches us that there will always remain a dynamic boundary of ignorance. My thesis is that this construct conveys a spiritual message to humankind appropriate to the modern era. This profound message is that, while we have received this enormous divine gift of science, human achievement needs to be tempered by the realization that there is a divine realm beyond the reach of the scientifically analyzable universe.

I have also been struck on my science-religion journey on the need to address another challenge to theism which frequently clouds the atheism-theism debate—that of the anthropomorphic fallacies. These arise from anthropic interpretations of divine attributes and misinterpretations arising from biblical literalism. To avoid these errors, which arise from ascribing any finite, naturalistic, human attributes to the supernatural God, I am proposing the term "non-predicate theism." I do need to stress, however, that "non-predicate" qualifies the ideology of theism and, needless to say, does not relate to the predicate of the divine subject. Indeed, this book concerns itself with God's bounty to humankind, and to God's relationship and communication to humankind, as will be detailed in the forthcoming chapters. The concept of a non-predicate qualification to the ideology of theism stresses that there are no human-comprehensible predicates relating to God. I believe that the introduction of this idea should address the challenges arising from incorrect understandings of divine attributes, and the misleading literal interpretations of the Scriptures, not only by Bible critics but even by religious believers as well—this will be elaborated on in chapter 5.

The Book in Outline

I have structured this book to flow from the classical arguments for the existence of God to the science narratives of the natural world which create the questions of reality and meaning, and on to the responses to these questions from the revelations by the supernatural Creator. Chapter 1 presents the classical approaches to seek answers to the questions of God's existence. In chapters 2, 3, and 4, I have briefly outlined the current science narrative of what is known of the universe. Science can serve a dualistic role—on the one hand to provide naturalistic reasons behind the observable universe, without the need to call on a supernatural explanation. On the other hand, what I will take forward in the subsequent chapters is the idea that science, by explaining nature, creates the scaffolding for inquiring into a more profound meaning behind this grandeur, complexity, beauty, and synchrony of the world we live in. In the next two chapters, therefore, the discussion will look at responding to the questions that natural science-based knowledge poses. The content of these two chapters will examine what has been communicated from the supernatural domain—i.e., aspects of divine revelation. Chapter 5 will discuss what God is not, i.e., the misrepresentations and fallacies surrounding the attributes of God—what I have proposed to call non-predicate theism. Chapter 6 will then examine the forms of divine communication to humankind. Chapter 7 will be devoted to defending theism against the challenges from atheism. I have aimed to pull together the arguments for evidential theism through the science narrative, in the final chapter 8.

1

The Search for Truth

> The foundation of all foundations and the pillar of wisdom is to know that there is a primary being who brought into being all existence. All the beings of the heavens, the earth and what is between them came into existence only from the truth of His being.[1]
>
> —MOSES MAIMONIDES (1135–1204)

"Knowing" God?

THE MOST PROFOUND OF all questions is "Does God exist?" If so, is that being the personal monotheistic God of the Bible? What can we know of God? It is indeed a religious imperative to "know" God—the first of the Ten Commandments given to humankind is an unequivocal identification of the personal God of the monotheistic religions. Exod 20:2, 3 and Deut 5:6, 7 state clearly "I am the God your Lord who brought you out of the land of Egypt, the house of bondage: You shall have no other gods besides Me." On the other hand, the Scriptures also allude to humans being unable to know the essence of God. Moses, the greatest of all prophets in the Jewish tradition, begged God, "Oh, let me behold Your presence!" (Exod 33:18) but was privileged only to see God's allegorical "back" from a cleft in the rock. " . . . you cannot see My face, for man may not see Me and live" (Exod 33:20). The concealment from humankind of the Divine, and other supernatural phenomena, is

---

1. Maimonides, *Yesodei HaTorah*, 1:1.

illustrated in the well-known Talmudic apologue of the four sages who resolved to enter the Pardes (a spiritual dimension in proximity to God).[2] After this exposure only one sage managed to emerge unscathed; of the remaining three, one died instantly, one become insane, and one become a heretic. Direct knowledge of God would conflict with the theological requirement for humans to have true freewill rather than living as a reward-and-punishment robot. Furthermore it would be logically incompetent for the created to have full knowledge of the creator. Logic dictates that a system cannot have knowledge from within.

The alternative approach of acquiring a knowledge of reality is to focus exclusively on science, an approach expressed as physicalism or materialism, which accepts that the material universe represents the totality of reality.[3] With the burgeoning of scientific knowledge from the early twentieth century onwards came the verification principle enunciated by the thinkers of the Vienna Circle.[4] They held that any statement is considered to be factual only if confirmed by sensory experience or mathematical calculation.[5] Some two centuries earlier, David Hume had put it more bluntly, enunciating that something which wasn't mathematically underwritten, abstract reasoning, or experimentally demonstrable, should be destroyed, as it was merely deception.[6] Is the probing mind searching for answers to reality satisfied with this materialistic monism in the era of twenty-first-century science? The challenge of materialistic atheism and its relationship to science will be discussed more fully in chapter 7. From the theist's standpoint, the challenge is to address the seemingly contrasting scriptural injunction to "know" God and the factuality that humankind is not empowered to know God's "face" or

2. b Chagigah 14b.

3. Stoljar, "Physicalism."

4. The Vienna Circle was a school of logical empiricism, comprised of philosophers, natural scientists, and social scientists, who met at the University of Vienna between 1924 and 1936.

5. Schlick, "Meaning and Verification."

6. See Hume, "Enquiry Concerning Human Understanding," 23.

anything of his essence. God remains hidden from humankind—"*Deus Absconditus.*"[7] What then are the approaches to seeking "knowledge" of God, and how may the idea of non-predicate theism contribute to support belief in God?

The Classical Philosophical Arguments

The three classical philosophical arguments for the existence of God—the cosmological, the ontological, and the teleological—are generally not widely accepted today in their original forms. Elements of these ideas, however, do still have some resonance in contemporary philosophy, as well as in the concept of non-predicate theism. Cosmological arguments focus on the regress of causal relationships responsible for the existence of the world; the teleological on the examination and the inference drawn from the special features of the world; and the ontological argument reflects on the concept of God.

1. The Cosmological Arguments

Also known as the Kalam cosmological arguments (after the group of Middle Ages Islamic scholars called the Mutakallimun). This family of arguments is based on inferences drawn from a regress chain of causal relationships, coupled with the denial of this chain being infinite. The incomprehensibility of the concept of infinity is key to the cosmological argument. In other words, the interruption of the regress because of the non-acceptance of an infinite regress, means that there is a first cause—the uncaused cause, which, theologically, is identified to be God. Four types of regress chains were described by St. Thomas Aquinas (1225–1274),[8] and comprise, respectively, the arguments from causation itself, the arguments from motion, the arguments from contingency, and the arguments from degrees. For each of these regress chains, the

7. Reinhuber, "Deus Absconditus/Deus Revelatus."
8. McInerney and O'Callaghan, "Saint Thomas Aquinas."

initiator of the chain, i.e., God, is defined as the first or uncaused cause, the unmoved mover, the necessary entity, or the pinnacle of perfection, respectively. A century earlier the Jewish philosopher and theologian, Moses Maimonides (1135–1204), had rationalised along similar lines that all events have causation and, therefore, need a prime mover who necessarily must be outside of the physical, as creation is a physical activity.[9]

Challenges and support for the cosmological arguments have come from classical and contemporary thinkers. Immanuel Kant (1724–1804) laid out several criticisms including the fact that, as it stands, the cosmological arguments fail to identify that the initiating author of the chain of causation is God or possibly even a committee of gods. There also remains, he asserted, the question of who or what caused God.[10] Kant also questioned whether existence or "being" is a predicate. David Hume (1711–1776) went further, querying the idea of a necessary existence, which is what links the elements of the chain of causation.[11] In other words, whenever we conceive of the existence of something, we can also conceive of its non-existence, and thus necessary existence has no meaning. In defence of the cosmological argument, Gottfried Wilhelm Leibniz (1646–1716) proposed that a fact or an object must have a reason or a cause—what he called "the principle of sufficient reason."[12] As the universe is an object, it must therefore have a reasonable cause—the first reason or cause of the universe being God. The contemporary Christian philosopher William Lane Craig (1949–) has proposed an advancement on the cosmological argument—whatever exists must have a cause; therefore as the universe began to exist it has a cause, and that cause is God.[13] However, quantum physics has countered these arguments, purporting to show that things can indeed come from nothing.[14] The multiverse hypothesis

9. See Maimonides, *Guide for the Perplexed*, 2:22,192–95.
10. Jankowiak, "Immanuel Kant."
11. See Hume, "Dialogues Concerning Natural Religion," 63.
12. Melamed and Lin, "Principal of Sufficient Reason."
13. Craig, *Kalam Cosmological Argument*.
14. Krause, *Universe from Nothing*.

(see chapter 4, pgs. 63–64) also challenges Craig's argument that there is a finite beginning of the universe, i.e., the Big Bang. Perhaps the most fundamental imponderable in the cosmological arguments is the concept of infinity itself, as all forms of this argument are grounded on the finite interruption of the regress, because of a denial of infinity. Is there a reality to infinity? The idea of something having no limit and no quantifiable measurement has been speculated on as far back as the pre-Socratic Greek philosophers, such as Anaximander (c. 610–546 CE), as well as the ancient Indian mathematicians.[15] The notion of infinity has been explored in philosophy, logic, computing, cosmology, physics, and, of course, mathematics. Despite the exactitude of mathematical analysis, infinity remains essentially an unbounded abstract. Hilbert's famous thought experiment of the paradox of the Grand Hotel[16] demonstrates that infinity cannot be treated like regular quantifiable numbers, and that infinity can create paradoxes of statements, which go as far as being counterintuitive, while being true. Does the concept of infinity belong to the same category of concepts that humankind lacks the ability to precisely define and quantify—concepts such as "always," "never," "unbounded space and time," etc.? The failure to definitively comprehend the reality of infinity does weaken its challenge to the denial of an infinite regress, which is a pivotal component of the cosmological argument.

15. Wikipedia, "Infinity."
16. The paradox of Hilbert's Grand Hotel is a thought experiment devised by the German mathematician David Hilbert (1862–1943). Briefly, it imagines a hotel with an infinite number of rooms, everyone occupied. To accommodate a new guest each existing guest moves up one room, room 1 to room 2, room 2 to room 3, and so on to infinity, and the new guest then occupies the vacated room 1. If an infinite number of new guests arrive they are accommodated by each existing guest moving up to a room number which is double their existing number, i.e., n to 2n. This frees up an infinite number of odd numbered rooms for the infinite number of new guests. The thought experiment is designed to demonstrate that a counterintuitive result can be shown to be true, i.e., even if every room is already occupied, any number of new guests can be accommodated, even an infinite number. It could also suggest that infinity is countable, as there's always additional rooms available for any number of new guests.

2. The Teleological Arguments

These are also referred to as arguments from purpose. They essentially propose that a reasoning and perceptive observer of the universe cannot fail to appreciate that, with all its complexity and beauty, the universe was intentionally assembled with purpose in mind. The design argument comes in two forms—design as purpose and design as regularity.

The design as purpose argument conceived by William Paley (1743–1805) is also called the argument by analogy.[17] Paley drew the analogy of the purposeful design in a human-manufactured watch to that of the creation of the eye, or indeed the creation of the natural world. There have been many and varied criticisms of the argument by design. Firstly, there is the criticism of the analogy itself. Paley's analogy infers a similarity of purpose between a human intentional artifact, like a watch, and natural phenomena. There are, however, numerous examples in the natural world that exist with no manifest purpose. With other examples the purpose could be construed to be purely a human figment of speculation rather than having any true purpose. Humans are amusingly characterised as being promiscuous teleologists—i.e., having the tendency to ascribe purpose to phenomena even where a purpose does not exist. Hume has also pointed to the numerous phenomena of the natural world, which could be termed "mistakes" such as natural disasters, which would imply a flawed creator. However, it was essentially the advent of Darwinian evolutionary theory, a half century after Paley, and the subsequent vast expansion of the science of evolutionary biology, which provided the scientifically verifiable knowledge of the mechanisms of life, and the development of species by random mutation and natural selection. And yet, a number of ever-present "loose ends" remain, and may well always be present to challenge a fully mechanistic explanation of all natural phenomena. In addition, there are clearly essential aspects of the living universe beyond the purely material. This, as

---

17. Davies, *Introduction to Philosophy of Religion*, 75.

well as the fine-tuning of the cosmos, hints at purpose. These issues will be dealt with more fully in chapter 3, see pg. 60.

A recent variation of the teleological argument is the design as regularity from Richard Swinburne (1934–), which posits that the clearly highly ordered universe is not accommodated by scientific explanation alone, and infers intention by an intelligent agency.[18] He has also advanced the argument from probability—that the Divine creation of the universe is the most likely of explanations (although this has been subject to the criticism of categorical error).

3. The Ontological Argument

This argument is generally associated with the *Proslogion* of St. Anselm of Canterbury (1033–1109) and differs conceptually from the cosmological and teleological arguments.[19] It proposes an *a priori* argument for the existence of God starting from a definition of the existence of God, i.e., what God is purported to be, rather than arguing proofs for the existence of God. Anselm thus defined God as "that than which nothing greater can be conceived." The argument posits that something exists in truth if it is not only imagined to exist but it goes beyond just being imagined, and on to reality. That is, it is a fact if it is not only an intellectual activity but exists also in reality. The argument was criticized, amongst others, by a contemporary of Anselm's, the Benedictine monk Guanilo, who countered that on the basis of Anselm's argument anything possible could be imagined to be real—even a fabulous island. St. Thomas Aquinas also rejected the notion that God's existence could be inferred from the concept of God. Immanuel Kant rejected the ontological argument as it was based on the issue of existence, which is an existentialist affirmation, and not a predicate—i.e., it does not assign qualitative characteristics to a subject. Contemporary Christian philosopher Alvin Plantinga (1932–) has

---

18. Swinburne, *Existence of God*.
19. Sadler, "Anselm of Canterbury."

attempted to salvage the ontological argument by putting forward the concept of a being with maximal greatness.[20]

The classical arguments for the existence of God have generally failed to convince most philosophers as well as many theologians. While they were influential in their time, today they are much less effective in withstanding the challenges from critics or modern non-believers. However teleology may still play a significant role in supporting religious belief. The science of cosmology has revealed an exquisitely fine-tuned universe seemingly pointing to purposeful design, with the only physicalist non-design response, that of the multiverse, being poorly defensible—see chapter 3, see pgs. 63–64. Similarly, biological evolution has produced extensively validated scientific evidence of selection in the process of speciation, but considerations of the wide complexity of the drives to achieve genetic advantage may also appear to point to intentional purpose rather than purely materialist mechanisms. These will be dealt with more fully in chapter 3, see pgs. 53–54.

Non-evidential Faith

For many theologians, knowledge of God through rational reasoning, observation of nature, and scientific investigation, i.e., what is referred to as natural theology, has not been able to provide a fully satisfactory foundation for religious belief. It is also axiomatic that, from a theological perspective, attempts by finite humans to acquire knowledge of the creator would, in any event, be futile. The need for this lack of knowledge is a fundamental religious requirement for unencumbered freewill, untainted by any robotic reward and punishment influence. As King Solomon, the wisest of all men, stated in Eccl 3:10–11:

> I have observed the business that God gave man to be concerned with: He brings everything to pass precisely at its time; He also puts eternity in their mind, but without

---

20. Plantinga, "Is Belief in God Properly Basic," 41–51.

man ever guessing, from first to last, all the things that God brings to pass.

Natural theology has also been criticized for objectifying religion into a clinical soulless mechanistic exercise. Soren Kierkegaard (1813–1855) has pointed out that faith in God should not merely be the accumulation of empirical observations and logical arguments; faith is a matter of individual subjective passion, which cannot be mediated by the clergy or by human artifacts.[21]

Fideism

The dependence on faith as a basis for religious belief in place of reason has been an important component of Christianity since the days of the early church fathers. One of the earliest of the Christian fideists, Tertullian (c. 160–230 CE), is perhaps best known for his maxim when referring to the Trinity and the incarnation: "*prosus credible est, quia ineptum est,*" translated as "it is by all means to be believed, because it is incongruous."[22]

Fideism as a religio-philosophical concept is generally associated with four philosophers, Pascal, Kierkegaard, James, and Wittgenstein, each contributing an individualistic variation on the general idea of religious truth through faith rather than reason.

Blaise Pascal the French mathematician-philosopher (1623–1662) is perhaps best known for articulating Pascal's Wager[23]—a pragmatic approach to fideism. Drawing up a 2 X 2 table, he showed that it is ultimately in one's best interest to believe in God in order to avoid punishment in hell if God did in fact exist, and one chose not to believe in Him.[24] Pascal's Wager, however, is in

21. McDonald, "Soren Kierkegaard."
22. Christianity, "credo quia absurdum."
23. Pascal's Wager

	BELIEVER	NON-BELIEVER
GOD EXISTS	Eternal Reward	Eternal Punishment
GOD DOES NOT EXIST	Neutral	Neutral

24. Amesbury, "Fideism."

reality more of a recommendation of expedience rather than a rationalized proof.

After Pascal, Soren Kierkegaard—to whom has been ascribed the aphorism "leap of faith"—was one of the earlier advocates of fideism. While Kierkegaard still maintained the compatibility of faith and reason, he viewed faith itself, not as unreasonable or irrational, but rather as being beyond the scope of philosophical reasoning.[25] He gave as a prime example of unfettered faith the biblical narrative of the willingness of Abraham to sacrifice his son Isaac.

William James (1842–1910) was a prominent defender of belief in the absence of proof—countering his contemporary well-known opponent W. K. Clifford (1845–1879). The latter outspokenly held that it was wrong and harmful to ever, under any circumstances, believe in something if not supported by sufficient evidence.[26] Countering Clifford, James defended the concept that belief was reasonable, even in the absence of proof.[27] So, for example, there are often situations in life when momentous choices need to be made and one feels unable to exercise free voluntary control—referred to as doxastic involuntarism.[28] These pragmatic decisions, which play a vital role in our lives, require belief without proof. One such momentous decision is the God decision.

Ludwig Wittgenstein (1889–1951), although not himself religious in the generally accepted sense, nevertheless espoused religiously sensitive views.[29] In this respect, like Kierkegaard, he regarded religion as practice rather than theory. Wittgensteinian fideism, as it came to be known, laid out a number of parameters including: the logical dissociation of religion from the other components of life; that religious dialogue, being self-referential,

---

25. Kierkegaard, *Fear and Trembling*.
26. Clifford, *Ethics of Belief*.
27. James, *Will to Believe*.
28. Doxastic = related to belief. Doxastic involuntarism (Hume) means inability to control one's belief as against doxastic voluntarism. Qu, "Doxastic Involuntarism," 53–92.
29. Nielsen, "Wittgensteinian Fideism," 191–209.

precludes talk of reality; and that beliefs are understood only by religious believers.

In the ensuing years, fideism's thesis that faith overrides reason came to be somewhat derogated, because of the perception that it rejected reason as a component of religious belief. In recent years contemporary philosophers John Bishop[30] and C. Stephen Evans,[31] amongst others, came to the defence of fideism by pointing out that not only did it not reject reason but in fact, reasoning is supported and promoted as a component of fideism. To clarify—what is rejected is the obligatory requirement for evidence in order for belief to be regarded as rational. Evidentialism is denied—in other words, the rationality of fideism is based on the fact that it is super-evidential—beyond the need for evidential support.[32]

Contemporary Christian philosopher Alvin Plantinga, in considering the question whether non-evidential belief in God is basic, has advanced the term "reformed epistemology."[33] He has argued that knowledge of God is direct and immediate, i.e., it is properly basic and foundational. He gives examples of other intuitive, immediate, and obvious foundational beliefs such as the awareness of loved ones, which evoke an immediate sensory experience. These beliefs are likewise accepted not on the basis of evidence. Awareness of God would similarly be just such an intuitive, non-inferential belief—the so-called *"sensus divinitatus."* These non-evidential beliefs are epistemically warranted and indefeasible and have come to be referred to as "the neo-foundationalism of Plantinga."

Other arational belief systems such as quasi-fideism have also been proposed—which similarly call for the same epistemic evaluation of religious belief, as is the case for other non-evidential beliefs.[34] Non-evidential or arational belief systems become vulnerable to the attack that they are a "copout"—a failure to reason the existence of God, and may receive criticism that their basis for belief

30. Bishop, *Believing by Faith*.
31. Evans, *Faith Beyond Reason*.
32. Kierkegaard, *Fear and Trembling*.
33. Plantinga, "Is Belief in God Properly Basic," 41–51.
34. Pritchard, "Wittgensteinian Quasi-Fideism," 145–59.

rests on emotional criteria. Are emotions to be trusted, as they are influenced in one extreme by charismatic ecstasy, or may be bolstered by the material trappings of ritual? Modern religious belief has come to be largely based on non-evidential faith. However, the religious convictions of thinking individuals which are based solely on non-evidential faith and unaccompanied by supporting rational ideation remain precarious. Relationships to phenomena which are based on emotional appeal alone are susceptible to failure if the drive which compelled the initial religious conviction decays. Deep reflection may see belief as an idea, rather than as a truth. Questions, challenges, and doubts may arise when the attributions of God are scrutinized in depth (hence the motivation for the proposed "non-predicate theism"—to be discussed in chapter 5).

Non-evidential Belief in the Jewish Tradition

Judaism had incorporated into its theology relatively little of what is generally understood to be western philosophy. The Orthodox Jewish religion is primarily based on *halacha*, which is the canon of Jewish law derived from the Holy Scriptures, the direct word of God, also referred to as the written law and the oral law. The oral law, which is of equal status to the written law, was also directly communicated by God to Moses, in order for it to be passed on to the Jewish nation into the future. (This will be discussed more fully in chapter 6 in relation to divine revelation as it pertains to the Jewish faith.) Certainly in its earliest stages, Jewish religion centered essentially on the temple and its attendant sacrifices. Following the destruction of both temples, worship was transferred to synagogues and sacrifices were replaced by the daily prayers.

The major engagements of Jewish philosophy essentially began in the pre-Middle Age Gaonic period, but predominated in the Middle Ages, with contributions coming from Jewish philosophers living mainly in Spain and North Africa. This was largely the Jewish response to the resuscitation of ancient Greek philosophy by Arab scholars of that time. The most famous philosophical work coming out of that era was *The Guide for the*

Perplexed by Moses Maimonides, written essentially along rationalist philosophical lines, and directed to negative theology (to be discussed in chapter 5, see pgs. 90–91).[35] In contrast, medieval poet-philosopher Rabbi Yehudah HaLevi (1075–1141), author of one of the most cherished books in Judaism, the *Kuzari*, laid emphasis on non-evidential faith: "When it comes to serving God, one cannot rely on logic, inference, or discretion."[36]

Jewish contributions advancing non-evidential faith have been published by contemporary rabbinic philosophers since the latter part of the last century. Rabbi Joseph B. Soloveitchik (1903–1993), in his famous work *The Lonely Man of Faith*, describes two different kinds of human being analogous to the narrative of the creation of humans in Gen 1 and Gen 2, respectively; Adam 1, described in chapter 1, also referred to as majestic man, may fit more into the natural theology mold, while Adam 2, in chapter 2, also referred to as covenantal man, corresponds to the non-evidential faith mold.[37] Rabbi Soloveitchik defends the idea of non-evidential faith:

> The trouble with all rational demonstrations of the evidence of God, with which the history of philosophy abounds, consists in their being exactly what they were meant to be by those who formulated them: abstract logical demonstrations divorced from the living primal experiences in which these demonstrations are rooted.[38]

In his work *Halachic Man*, Rabbi Soloveitchik similarly contrasts these two types of individuals as cognitive man, linked to empirical reality and scientific understanding, and religious man, who ventures past the concrete physical realm.[39] A recent publication by Rabbi Aharon Lichtenstein (1933–2015) conveys the same idea in his essay "The Source of Faith is Faith Itself."[40]

---

35. Maimonides, *Guide for the Perplexed*.
36. HaLevi, *Kuzari*, 121.
37. Soloveitchik, *Lonely Man of Faith*,
38. Soloveitchik, *Lonely Man of Faith*, 49.
39. Soloveitchik, *Halachic Man*.
40. Lichtenstein, "Source of Faith," 188–91.

2

Science and Meta-Science

> How much can we know of the world? Can we know everything? Or are there fundamental limits to how much science can explain . . . of physical reality?[1]
>
> —MARCELO GLEISER

Science and the Search for Truth

FOR CENTURIES, HUMANKIND HAS sought the truth, through science by studying nature, through philosophy by the study of reason, and through religion by the study of doctrine and faith. For some, this endeavor has been restricted to only one of these three avenues of inquiry, while others have sought to integrate all three. Some ten centuries ago, the great Middle-Ages theologian, scientist, and philosopher, Moses Maimonides, understood the importance of science for the support of religious faith " . . . nothing can be predicated of God . . . In this respect our knowledge of God is aided by the study of Natural Science."[2]

But he nevertheless cautioned that:

> . . . a boundary is undoubtedly set to the human mind which it cannot pass. There are things (beyond that boundary) which are acknowledged to be inaccessible to human understanding, and man does not show any desire to comprehend them, being aware that such

---

1. Gleiser, *Island of Knowledge*, xiii.
2. Maimonides, *Guide for the Perplexed* 1:55, 78.

knowledge is impossible, and that there are no means of overcoming the difficulty.[3]

Today, at the end of the second decade of the twenty-first century, despite the vast expanse of scientific knowledge, there does still remain great gaps of knowledge of the natural world. Will there always be a perpetually moving frontier of knowledge, or an endlessly receding so-called cosmic horizon of knowledge, beyond which stretches the great terrain of the unknown?[4] I would posit that the history of scientific progress demonstrates a distinctive pattern of a perpetual knowledge barrier, which thereby supports the notion of a supernatural reality beyond the physical world.

The Tools of Science

Scientific investigation is pursued through five interactive, non-exclusive pathways of inquiry:

1. Descriptive/Observational Inquiry—the analysis and interpretation of observed phenomena, for example, much of the paleontological and cosmological sciences.

2. Mathematical/Extrapolative Inquiry—mathematics is often described as the incontrovertible science. However, mathematical extrapolations do on occasion lead to abstract insensate concepts, such as infinity.

3. Experimental Inquiry—activities created to demonstrate and establish a truth by means of planned experiments, and validated by means of competent controls, repeatability, and falsifiability.

4. Inference to the Best Explanation—developing a hypothesis which would explain specific phenomena if they were true. Applications of inference to the best explanation range from clinical and epidemiological conclusions in the medical sciences to the Higgs boson in the physical sciences.

---

3. Maimonides, *Guide for the Perplexed* 1:31, 41.
4. Gleiser, *Island of Knowledge*.

5. **Speculation**—non-evidence-based hypothesizing an answer to a particular scientific question. For example, the multiverse hypothesis—to be discussed in chapter 3, see pgs. 63–64.

The Methodology of Science

Table 1: The Flow of Scientific Investigation

Status of Scientific Knowledge	Interpretation of Findings
1. Preliminary findings	Tentative
2. Repeatability of findings	Changes are frequent
3. Broad conclusions	Changes do occur regularly
4. Scientific concepts	Changes occur only occasionally
5. Scientific facts	Changes are rare
6. Scientific laws and principles	Changes at this stage are very rare
7. Scientific theories	Foundational but not totally immutable

The confidence of the scientific method to produce authentic, evidence-based truths is underpinned by its rigor and meticulousness, as well as the competence of its control tools, which are built into the scientific method. This is best illustrated by the mechanics of the scientific method as applied to experimental inquiry. The modus operandi, here, is generally formed of three phases—a planning phase, a testing phase and a formulation phase.

1. The planning phase frames the question of the scientific inquiry. The research question would be an attempt to explain an observation, or it could be a deduction, or an extrapolation, or a contestation of existing knowledge. These questions would generally be derived from published scientific literature. An open-ended question is constructed and a hypothetical answer to the question is postulated. The investigation would need to build in to the planning, firstly, how a predicted outcome could be falsified by counterevidence, and, secondly, what the consequences would be of the postulated results.

2. The testing phase aims to determine the outcome and implications of the postulated results. The design of the experimental phase must ensure that suitable controls are incorporated. In other words, while the testing is specific rather than broad, the controls need to be broad and not specific, in order to address confounders or potential sources of bias. After adequate validation with tools such as statistics, the results are analyzed as to their meaning. In the scientific world the findings would be subject to peer review and publication in a recognized scientific journal, in order for the experimental outcome to be further authenticated by its repeatability by scientists in other laboratories.

3. Formulation of these findings into scientific knowledge is the final phase of the scientific process. This progresses through a series of steps. Preliminary findings are, of course, tentative. Once they are reliably repeated, broad conclusions can be drawn, although changes in details, and even scope, do occasionally occur. Scientific concepts related to these findings then follow, but even at this stage revisions and changes to these findings do still sometimes arise. Scientific facts are then developed—at this stage changes are rare. This leads on to the development of scientific laws and principles—content changes now would be very rare, but certainly do occur from time to time.

The term "theory" in the scientific world conveys a meaning that is diametrically opposed to that used in everyday language. Common usage of "theory" connotes possibility or uncertainty, while in science the word "theory" is definitive and means the assembly of scientific facts, laws, and principles to explain natural phenomena (for example the atomic theory, the germ theory, etc). The usual follow-on from these investigations is the generation of new research questions that frame further avenues of inquiry. Along the way new scientific knowledge may well spawn technological offshoots such as medical interventions and industrial applications.

The Scientific Method Versus the Religious Quest for Truth

Table 2: The Scientific Process vs. the Religious Process

Science	Religion
Content neutral	Content based on revelation or authority
No pre-conceived conclusions	Conclusions based on faith. Religion essentially forbids deviation from creed
Disprove claims—purposively seeks counterevidence which may modify or reject claims	Claims are inviolable despite the possibility of counterevidence
Makes predictions based on scientific knowledge	Predictions may be based on prophecy

From the above detail it is clear that scientific knowledge is derived from a systematic process with built-in verification and validation tools, which provide the assurance for authentic information of the natural world. Science has enjoyed enormous success in unlocking many of the secrets of the universe. It has facilitated the harnessing of nature to promote the well-being of humankind and it has provided technology to improve the quality of human life. Nevertheless, science, being a human construct, is limited in the extent of its investigative abilities and its elucidation of reality. Moreover, the fundamental question remains—is there a reality beyond the physical? As the theologian and philosopher Abraham Joshua Heschel (1907–1972) pointed out:

> The moment we utter the name of God we leave the level of scientific thinking and enter the realm of the ineffable. Such a step is one which we cannot take scientifically, since it transcends the boundaries of all that is given. It is in spite of all warnings that man has never ceased to be stirred by ultimate questions. Science cannot silence him, because scientific terms are meaningless to

the spirit that raises these questions, meaningless to the concern for a truth greater than the world that science is engaged in exploring.[5]

Science and/or Religion

1. Polarization of Positions

There can be very few people who can fail to admit the success and the value of the scientific endeavor to humanity. Nevertheless, on both ends of the spectrum of the science and religion argument many people adopt rejectionist positions:

Science rejection—There are sizeable populations of conservative religious persuasion, in many countries throughout the world, who "reject" science (although there is seldom a reticence to benefit from the benefits and conveniences that science-based technology and medicine offer). Suspicion of science is especially marked with regard to evolutionary biology and its related sciences, and even more so with respect to the evolution of humankind. A recent *Gallup* poll reported that some 38 percent of Americans are of the belief that humans were created in their present form by God less than 10,000 years ago.[6]

Religion rejection—The populations of non-believers/atheists also represent sizeable numbers who reject religion, asserting that all reality supervenes on the physical,[7] and all knowledge of the world is explicable, or will be explicable in the future, by science. (These issues relating to non-belief will be addressed in chapter 7.)

Both ends of the spectrum have extremist intolerant standpoints, whether it is religious fundamentalist rejection of science,

---

5. Heschel, *God in Search of Man*, 102.
6. Swift, "Belief in Creationism."
7. Stoljar, "Physicalism."

or the militant, evangelical, "new atheist" disparaging of religion as being "comparable to the smallpox virus but harder to eradicate."[8]

2. Partition—Non-overlapping Magisteria

Usually abbreviated as NOMA. This proposal was put forward by the biologist Stephen Jay Gould[9] (1941–2002). It suggests that there is no conflict between science and religion as they pursue quite different domains of inquiry. While science is involved in elucidating mechanisms, i.e., the "how" of nature, religion concerns itself with the "why" questions—morals, ethics and values. At first this approach would appear to promote an elegant and harmonious relationship between science and religion, each compartmentalized to their separate interests, concerns, and routes of inquiry. Science concerns itself with how the physical world works, and religion with the "why" questions—the reason behind all these truths and the spiritual concepts of morality, ethics, and values. Seemingly each endeavor would be confined to its own terms of interest with no overlap. However, far from this ideal, the reality is that there is indeed considerable overlap—science does study religion, while religious thought and interests are very much involved with science. (Indeed, in the introduction, see pg. 1, a plea was made for greater involvement of philosophy and theology in the pursuit of science.) In the main, the concept of NOMA has not been widely accepted by scientists or theologians. Restriction of either intellectual pursuit to its exclusive and isolated compartment demeans and devalues both of them.

---

8 Dawkins, *"Is Science a Religion,"* 26–29. "It is fashionable to wax apocalyptic about the threat to humanity posed by the AIDS virus, 'mad cow' disease, and many others but I think a case can be made that faith is one of the world's great evils, comparable to the smallpox virus but harder to eradicate."

9 Gould, "Non-Overlapping Magisteria," 23.

3. Awe and Wonderment

This is probably the commonest response by most believers when asked why they believe in God. What modern science has revealed of the natural world can only be described in superlatives—the incredible diversity of life, the enormity of the universe, and the beauty, pageantry, and spectacle of nature is, to the theist, the confirmation of belief and the support for worship of the Almighty. Charles Darwin (1809–1882) himself so beautifully concluded in *The Origin of Species*:

> Thus, from the war of nature, from famine and death, the most exalted object which we are capable of conceiving, namely the production of the higher animals, directly follows. There is grandeur in this view of life, with its several powers, having been originally breathed by the Creator into a few forms or into one; and that, whilst this planet has gone cycling on according to the fixed law of gravity, from so simple a beginning endless forms most beautiful and most wonderful have been, and are being evolved.[10]

As mentioned above, the marvels of the natural world revealed by science constitute one element of the evidence for belief in God—the element of constituting the questions of meaning, which require a response that is supplied by the revelation of religion (see chapter 6). However, to the non-believing skeptic and in particular the atheist, fascination with the enormity and beauty of nature, as awe-inspiring as it may well be, deserves to be admired and appreciated but does not constitute evidence for the existence of God.

---

10. Darwin, *Origin of Species*, 425. The original edition of the book omitted the words "having been originally breathed by the Creator." To forestall the anticipated outcry from the religious public of Victorian England, and especially from his devout wife Emma Wedgwood, Darwin inserted the phrase into subsequent editions of the book.

4. Utilizing Science to Authenticate Scripture

There have been attempts by several religious scientists to utilize scientific knowledge to directly align with segments of the Scriptures, such as the age of the universe. For example, Gerald Schroeder's *Genesis and the Big Bang*[11] and Nathan Aviezer's *In the Beginning*[12] are such attempts. In these and other books, the authors using the tools of science claim to demonstrate reconciliation of biblical accounts of creation of the universe, and the creation of humans, with modern scientific knowledge. These exercises may provide some interesting insights,[13] but as "proofs" of the scientific veracity of the scriptural accounts of the creation of the universe, they are vulnerable not only to challenges of their scientific correctness,[14] but also that, in time, these assertions may be undermined by new scientific insights and knowledge.

5. God of the Gaps

The God of the gaps is a common but mistaken defense for belief in God. It relies on the many gaps in current scientific knowledge of the natural world, and on the assumption that these gaps will never be elucidated by science. These gaps in the scientific explanations of natural phenomena therefore seem to belong outside of the natural and in the realm of the divine, and are used as proof of the existence of God. However, this line of reasoning is problematic as "gaps" have a habit of eventually being filled in as scientific knowledge advances. As mentioned in the introduction, see pgs. 5–6, "god of the gaps" was spoken of as far back as the ancient Greeks, by the physician Hippocrates:

There have been many modern examples of the shortcomings of the "god of the gaps" argument. An illustrative example until late into the twentieth century concerned the seeming cul-de-sac of a

11. Schroeder, *Genesis and the Big Bang*.
12. Aviezer, *In the Beginning*.
13. Perakh, "End of the Beginning."
14. Perakh, "Confronted with Critique."

possible scientific explanation for abiogenesis (the origin of life). The developing science of molecular biology in the mid-twentieth century had revealed that DNA constituted the genetic material necessary to code for proteins, the structural building blocks of the body as well as the enzymes that are required, *inter alia*, for the replication of DNA. This created the conundrum of how life could have originated naturally. If the first building blocks of life were proteins, there would be no mechanism for the genetic coding necessary for reproduction. On the other hand, if the first building blocks were nucleic acid (i.e., DNA) there would be no proteins to act as enzymes for the required assembly and replication of the DNA. This apparently insoluble scientific knowledge gap was, not surprisingly, eagerly seized on by many theologians. Here was a much-needed "scientific" indicator that a supernatural God was needed who could produce both of these organic chemical building blocks simultaneously, and then to functionally integrate them with each other to allow for the first forms of life to develop. The abiogenesis conundrum came to be a prime example of the "god of the gaps" argument. However, the more recent characterization of the properties of RNA (ribonucleic acid)—the nucleic acid used by DNA to transcribe proteins, revealed that RNA could not only code for proteins (indeed in the case of the RNA viruses it is the sole repository of its genetic material), but, in addition, that it had enzymatic and regulatory properties which would be necessary for effective reproduction. This came to be known as the RNA-world hypothesis.[15] The RNA-world hypothesis provided a very plausible hypothesis for RNA being the original molecule of life, acting both as a repository of the genetic code and also as an enzyme for the replication of the nucleic acid, and thereby undermining this "god of the gaps" example.

---

15. Joyce, "Antiquity of RNA-based Evolution," 214–21. Kun et al., "Dynamics of the RNA World," 75–95. Schiller, "Mini-Motif Synthesis," 289–96.

Is There a Religious Message in Meta-Science?

Is the process of how science advances knowledge of the natural world, i.e., meta-science, sending out a message of religious relevance? Marcelo Gleiser (1959–) in his book *The Island of Knowledge* shows how scientific research, as impressive as its gains have been, always encounters a barrier to further knowledge—"the limits of science"—which serve to generate yet further questions.[16] It is indeed these further questions that are the fuel of scientific research, whose vastness is illustrated by a 2009 study from the University of Ottawa. That study found that there are approximately 2.5 million new scientific papers published annually in some 28,100 scholarly peer-reviewed journals.[17] The number of publishing scientists grew by about 4 to 5 percent per year! The scientific literature is so vast that today's researchers are compelled to utilize various information retrieval facilities and even machine learning and artificial intelligence techniques, in order to keep abreast of developments in their respective specialty.[18]

This dynamic pattern of a seemingly perpetual advance of research up to a knowledge barrier, but never reaching the finality of total knowledge, is reminiscent of the frustrating punishment meted out to the mythical king Sisyphus, sentenced by the gods for the sins of self-aggrandizement and deceit, and condemned to perpetually roll a boulder up a hill only for it to roll down again as he neared the summit. Is there a religious message, which emanates from a reality that lies beyond what science can ever reach? Is there a religious message in the Sisyphean nature of meta-science, a message that humans, with all their vast capabilities and enormous successes in unlocking the secrets of the universe and harnessing the benefits of science, will never have total understanding of the natural world? What lies behind this never-ending but constantly receding horizon of knowledge? Is the message that total knowledge belongs only to

---

16. Gleiser, *Island of Knowledge*.
17. Boon, "21st Century Science Overload."
18. NAS, *Reproducibility and Replicability*, 31.

that being who created the world, and not that single component of His creation, the human being?

To illustrate this Sisyphean pattern of the scientific narrative I will review, as an example, the meta-science of biological heredity. There are, of course, similar examples in the other sciences—I will touch on the insurmountable knowledge barrier in the cosmological science in the following chapter.

How are the Characteristics of Living Organisms Inherited?

Lamarckism

The first scientific attempt to understand the mechanism of heredity could be attributed to the work of the French naturalist Jean-Baptiste Lamarck (1744–1829). Lamarckism, as it came to be known, postulated that organisms acquired their heritable characteristics during their lifetime from use or disuse, in response to the challenges of the environment in which they found themselves. These acquired adaptive characteristics would then, it was thought, be passed on to their offspring and on to succeeding generations. The mechanisms of how these traits arose and how they were transmitted to descendants was, of course, completely unknown to Lamarck.

Darwinian Evolution and Heritable Traits

The epoch of biological sciences, as constituted today, essentially commenced on July 1, 1858, with a presentation of a paper to the Linnaean Society by the British naturalist Charles Darwin. This was followed a year later with the publication of his book, *The Origin of Species*.

The three pillars of Darwinian evolution—common ancestry, natural selection of advantageous traits, and heritable reproduction of these traits to succeeding generations, are conceptually charmingly simple. In fact, aspects of the evolution of species had been postulated, in some form, well before Darwin, by thinkers going all the way back to the ancient Greeks. But it was Darwin who scientifically systematized, analyzed, and supported the science of evolution with a vast amount of biological evidence, collected from his round-the-world voyage as the naturalist on the survey expedition of *HMS Beagle*. The mechanism of heredity was, however, at that time an unknown frontier. It was a contemporary of Darwin, the Austrian Augustinian friar, Gregor Johann Mendel (1822–1884), who first detailed the mechanics of inheritance of traits in plants. The understanding of the molecular mechanism of inheritance, a key to the evolution of species, was an unknown frontier of nineteenth-century science. Nucleic acid had been isolated from white blood cells by the Swiss physician Friedrich Miescher (1844–1895) but the function of the substance was not known at that time.

The Discovery of DNA and the Genetic Code

The first experimental demonstration of the transmission of genetic information was published in 1928 by the British bacteriologist, Frederick Griffith (1879–1941).[19] Working on the development of a vaccine against the prevalent cause of bacterial pneumonia, the pneumococcus, Griffith described two forms of the bacterium—a smooth form (producing smooth colonies when cultured on agar medium), which is lethal to laboratory mice, and a non-lethal, rough form. By mixing heat-killed smooth bacteria with live non-lethal bacteria, he demonstrated that the rough bacteria were transformed into the lethal form when tested in mice. In other words, genetic material from the heat-killed lethal form was transferred to the live non-lethal variety, providing it with the genetic coding for virulence. (Unlike the other constituents of the bacterium, DNA is not as affected by heat, and was therefore shown to be the repository of the gene for virulence.)

Some 16 years later, Oswald Avery (1877–1955), Colin MacLeod (1909–1972), and Maclyn McCarty (1911–2005), working

---

19. Griffith, *Significance of Pneumococcal Types*, 113–59.

at the Rockefeller Institute in New York, refined Griffith's experiment by purifying the constituent chemicals of bacteria and showing that indeed DNA was the transforming agent.[20] In 1952, Alfred Hershey (1908–1997) and Martha Chase (1927–2003) in Cold Spring Harbor in New York State further confirmed that the domicile of genetic information lay in DNA, through radioactive labeling of the proteins and nucleic acid of a bacterial virus (bacteriophage T2).[21]

Characterizing DNA and the Advent of Molecular Genetics

Now that DNA was identified as the chemical constituent of genetic information of living organisms, the new scientific frontier was to understand how it was structured, and how it transmitted the heritable characteristics to offspring. Using the then novel technique of x-ray diffraction crystallography, the British physical chemist Rosalind Franklin (1920–1958) was able to show that the DNA molecule was helical and formed a double helix structure by linking the sugar and phosphate molecules which form its backbone.[22] The x-ray diffraction photographs produced by Franklin laid the foundation of the understanding of the structure, and later the function, of the DNA molecule. The famous double helix structure of DNA was published as a single-page letter in the journal *Nature* in April 1953 by James Watson (1928–) and Francis Crick (1916–2004).[23] (They received the Nobel Prize in 1962.) The sequencing of the building blocks of DNA, the nucleotides, which form the long chain of the DNA molecule, followed soon after. The exact order of the nucleotides was predicted to be the key to the understanding of how the genetic code, enshrined in the DNA molecule, was able to specify the structure and function of living organisms—the next scientific frontier.

20. Avery et al., "Studies on the Chemical Nature," 137–58.
21. Hershey and Chase, "Independent Functions," 39–56.
22. Klug, "Rosalind Franklin," 808–10.
23. Watson and Crick, "Molecular Structure of Nucleic Acid," 737–38.

Initially DNA sequencing was a laborious and time-consuming process and impracticable for the sequencing of significant lengths of DNA. (A gene varies from several hundred to two million nucleotides in length.) Automated techniques were developed in the 1970s, and the first automated DNA sequencing machine was introduced towards the end of the 1980s. Today several instrument manufacturers produce machines, which are indispensable hardware in molecular genetic laboratories. What had previously taken months to sequence could now be achieved in seconds. In rapid succession came the identification of the sequence of thousands of genes in animals, plants, and humans, including the complete sequence of the genomes (the total genetic component) of many organisms. Genes could now be manipulated, transplanted, modified, and even artificially synthesized. Innumerable medical, agricultural, and industrial applications cascaded from the new science. Valuable proteins were produced by man-made genes, for example, vaccines against diseases such as hepatitis B and hormones such as insulin. Over 1,000 disease-causing genes have been identified, and gene therapy to treat genetic degenerative diseases of humans is rapidly becoming a reality. The recent advent of the powerful gene editing technology, CRISPR-Cas9 has been an extremely promising biomedical, agricultural, and industrial tool.[24] It has enabled rapid identification of specified genes, including disease-causing rogue genes, as well as being able to effectively excise and replace them. This very powerful new technology has aroused enormous excitement in the scientific world and opened up new knowledge frontiers.

In 1990, a multinational team headed by the National Institutes of Health of the USA, as well as a privately funded consortium, Celera Genomics, began the task of sequencing the three billion "letters" (i.e., nucleotides) of the human genome. The initial results of the project were published independently in February

---

24. De Buhr and Lebbink, "CRISPR to Combat Viral Infections," 123–29. Doudna and Charpentier, "New Frontier of Genetic Engineering," 0961–0969. Jaganathan et al., "CRISPR for Crop Improvement," 1–17. Singh et al., "Exploring the Potential," 1–18.

SCIENCE AND META-SCIENCE

2001 by the two groups in the journals *Nature* and *Science*, respectively.[25] The so-called "deciphering of the code of the human genome" will undoubtedly herald a new phase in our understanding of the fundamental molecular mechanisms of human heredity as well as the treatment of human disease.

As sophisticated and complex as the science of molecular genetics has become, it has now opened up many new frontiers of knowledge.

The New Horizons—Epigenetics

At the close of the twentieth century, science had delivered a vast storehouse of knowledge on the mechanisms of heredity. The universal site of genetic information for all forms of living things was now firmly established to be the DNA molecule, further supporting the one pillar of Darwinian evolution—that all life originated from a common ancestor. The detailed structure of the DNA molecule was now well-described as was the mechanism of how genetic information in DNA specifies the characteristics of living organisms. The puzzle of why nucleic acid, which consists of only four building blocks (nucleotides), turned out to be the repository of genetic information, rather than what had seemed to be more likely, proteins with their twenty-three building blocks (amino acids), was resolved. How the chain of nucleotides coded for structural proteins, enzymes, hormones, and other proteins, was now well understood, as well as the complexities involved in DNA transcription to the intermediary RNA, followed by the translation to the target protein. As a result of these advances, new knowledge boundaries opened up which led, in turn, to the birth of new challenges of understanding.

The first surprise was the discovery that the total number of genes in humans was much less than anticipated. Originally, it was estimated that the total number of human genes should be well over 100,000. However, to the great surprise of the scientific

---

25. International Human Genome Sequencing Consortium, "Initial Sequencing," 860–921. Venter et al., "Sequence of the Human Genome," 1304–51.

community, it was revealed by the human genome project that humans possess a mere 22,000 genes, not much more than the 20,000 genes in the well-studied and characterized genome of the lowly 1 millimeter-long roundworm, *Caenorhabditis elegans*. A second puzzle, in fact predating the Human Genome Project, was how each of the approximately 200 different types of cells in the human body, each carrying the same DNA genome, produce cells varying from liver cells to skin cells and brain cells. Thirdly, and perhaps most unexpectedly, the Human Genome Project revealed that only about 1 or 2 percent of genes actually code for proteins. The function of the remaining 98 percent of non-coding genes was, initially, beyond the frontier of knowledge. At the time these genes, which formed the great majority of the genome, were irreverently dubbed "junk genes." Advancing beyond that frontier, further research established that, far from being "junk," these non-coding genes played an essential role in the regulation of gene expression and, ultimately, the characteristics of the organism. Towards the end of the twentieth century and entering the twenty-first century, it became abundantly clear that the molecular mechanisms of heredity were vastly more complicated and also involved non-genetic heredity of structural and functional traits of organisms.

The science of epigenetics has flourished in the twenty-first century, and is now resolving many of the questions of transgenerational heredity, in particular, the role of environmental factors on heredity (resuscitating an interest in Lamarckism which had all but been discarded with the advent of Darwinism and Mendelian inheritance). Two landmark population studies demonstrated the definitive role of the environment on hereditary traits. The Dutch hunger study examined the offspring of mothers who had endured severe starvation in the Netherlands during the punitive Nazi-orchestrated famine of 1944–1945. These children, who were affected throughout their lives from the dietary deprivation of their mothers, experienced significantly higher rates of obesity, diabetes, and schizophrenia, and had a 10 percent increase in mortality after 68 years.[26] A contrasting finding,

---

26. Heijmans et al., "Persistent Epigenetic Differences," 17046–49.

but also an epigenetic effect of diet—this time glut, resulted in a marked reduction in longevity in the offspring of grandparents, who had been exposed to abundant food during cycles of famine and plenty in the nineteenth century, in Norrbotten, northern Sweden.[27] Epigenetics also addresses the question of why identical twins, with identical DNA genomes (coming from the same fertilized ovum), are not identical in physical, psychological, and other characteristics, as a result of environmentally induced differences, which affect the epigenome.[28]

Extensive investigations of the mechanisms of the epigenetic regulation of gene expression have shown that cells possess a basic genetic landscape from very early in embryonic development. Subsequent modifications occur through the regulation of gene expression by a process called methylation—where methyl molecules[29] attach to the DNA of genes and thereby modify their expression.[30] Another modifying mechanism involves histones, which are the amino acids of proteins responsible for the folding of the DNA in the chromosome. Attachment of various markers to the histone tails will affect either the tightness or the unfolding of the chromosome at a particular gene location—unfolded and exposed genes will display enhanced expression and vice versa. Many similar studies have investigated related epigenetic phenomena in non-human organisms. As an important agricultural example, the queen honeybee and her female workers share identical DNA sequences, but the radical differences in their structure and behavior has been shown to be due to methylation patterns of their genes.[31] Recent findings from population studies have now also shown how environmental challenges, for example, dietary factors,[32] or life in high altitudes

---

27. Byrgen, "Intergenerational Health Responses," 49–60.
28. Flintoff, "Identical Twins," 667.
29. The methyl group is a simple hydrocarbon molecule consisting of a carbon atom linked to three hydrogen atoms.
30. Dor and Cedar, "Principles of DNA Methylation," 1–8.
31. Lyko et al., "Honey Bee Epigenome," 1–12.
32. Hancock et al., "Human Adaptations to Diet," 8924–30.

with reduced oxygen[33] can result in epigenetic modifications, as well as adaptive mutations in the genome.

The sciences of molecular genetics, epigenetics, gene mapping, recombinant technology and others, have now resolved many of the erstwhile mysteries of the world of living organisms at the molecular level. As a spin-off, in the field of medicine, vast strides have been made in the understanding of aging, cancer and degenerative diseases. Most recently, next generation sequencing technology, which rapidly and precisely sequences almost the entire genome, is now being introduced into the clinical diagnostic laboratory. Much, however, still remains to be learned, and while epigenetics has been established as a discipline in its own right, an understanding of the details and the physiological role of the processes which are involved, remains beyond the present horizon of knowledge.[34]

The pageant of molecular genetics research is a typical illustration of the advancing horizon of scientific knowledge. The excitement of the unlocking of the structure of DNA in 1953 by Watson and Crick, promised a quick understanding of the mechanisms of gene function. Laborious manual sequencing, replaced by automated sequencing, reinforced an imminent expectation to wrap up the mysteries of the gene. The total sequencing of the human genome in 2001 was greeted with exultant jubilation. President Bill Clinton, on announcing the success of the Human Genome Project, exuded: ". . . today we are learning the language in which God created life."[35] However, this achievement served to reveal yet further horizons, for example, why there were only some 22,000 genes in the human genome of which only 2 percent code for proteins—what was the role of the 98 percent of the genome, initially termed "junk"? The role of epigenome now comes to the fore, and, in turn, its mysteries remain to be explored.

33. Pritchard et al., "Genetics of Human Adaptation," R208–R205.
34. Dor and Cedar, "Principles of DNA Methylation," 1–8.
35. Today in Science History: Https://todayinsci.com/C/Clinton_William/ClintonWilliam-CreationQuote800px.htm.

The science of genetics is but one example of what is so characteristic of all the sciences, historically and up to the present day. Throughout the world, hundreds of thousands of scientists are publishing millions of research articles in thousands of peer-reviewed journals[36] in order to explore the present frontiers of knowledge that have been structured from preceding scientific research. These current frontiers of knowledge will, in turn, generate even more frontiers to challenge future researchers, ad infinitum. The analogy of the marathon runner illustrates best the meta-science cycle. The runner aims for each milestone along the way and, on reaching it, looks ahead to the next milestone. But unlike the marathon runner, for the scientist the finishing line just keeps moving further down the road. Science, while it has become the intellectual idol of the atheist, it is still but a fraction of the reality of the creation. Science is unquestionably an immensely valuable gift from God, to be utilized for the benefit of humankind, but it also needs to be recognized within the true context that it occupies in the broader panoply of reality.

36. Boon, "21st Century Science Overload."

3

Design and Frontiers

> A common sense interpretation of the facts suggests that a super intellect has monkeyed with physics, as well as with chemistry and biology, and that there are no blind forces worth speaking about in nature. The numbers one calculates from the facts seem to me so overwhelming as to put this conclusion almost beyond question.[1]
>
> —Fred Hoyle (1915–2001), British astrophysicist

> I find it as difficult to understand a scientist who does not acknowledge the presence of a superior rationality behind the existence of the universe as it is to comprehend a theologian who would deny the advances of science.[2]
>
> —Wernher von Braun (1912–1977),
> pioneer rocket engineer

Revisiting the Teleological Argument

IN CHAPTER 1 WE briefly looked at the classical design argument of William Paley—the so-called argument by analogy (see pg. 16). The intricacy of a watch indicates that a designer was responsible and, by analogy, the far greater complexity of the natural world

---

1. Hoyle, "Universe," 16.
2. McIver, "Ancient Tales," 258–76.

would be indicative of a supernatural designer. The most important criticism of this argument came with the advent of Darwinian evolution, which began to provide natural explanations for the origin and development of living organisms. Towards the end of the nineteenth century, the science-religion debate was relatively simple. The science of the time, which was beginning to provide natural explanations for natural phenomena, supplied the non-believer with reason to dispense with the need for a supernatural creator. As the pace of discovery accelerated, so did the confidence of many scientists at the time that very soon all the outstanding unknowns of the natural world would be resolved. "There is nothing new to be discovered in physics now. All that remains is more and precise measurement," was stated in 1900, and attributed, disputably, to Lord Kelvin (1824–1907).[3] Similarly, in the biomedical sciences, even into the early twentieth century, the American medical historian Henry Sigerist (1891–1957), confidently asserted in 1931 that "Most of the infectious diseases . . . have now yielded up their secrets . . . Many illnesses . . . have been completely exterminated; [others had] been brought largely under control."[4] Some 40 years later William H. Stewart (1921–2008), the Surgeon General, told the United States Congress in 1969 that it was time to "close the book on infectious diseases."[5]

From the latter part of the twentieth century and firmly into the twenty-first century, the scientific endeavor had revealed a universe of staggering complexity, and yet, constructed from building blocks of extraordinary simplicity—the seventeen elementary particles and four fundamental forces; see below. At the same time, the advanced science of quantum physics had developed a world of complexity that perplexes virtually all who are not intimately

---

3. This quote has been attributed to Lord Kelvin in an address to the British Association for the Advancement of Science in 1900. There is, however, no record of his having said this precise quote. It may perhaps be a paraphrase of an earlier quote in 1894 by the physicist Albert A Michelson, " . . . it seems probable that most of the underlying principles have been firmly established."
4. Cohen, "Changing Patterns in Infectious Diseases," 762–67.
5. Spelberg, "Mistaken or Malignant," 294.

involved with that science.[6] What is the fundamental meaning of this deluge of new information? Does it strengthen the assertion that the natural world is explicable mechanistically, and not requiring any supernatural input? Or does the sheer enormity and the complexity of the structure of the universe strengthen the conviction that there is a divine creator who has conceived, created, governs, and maintains the universe? This chapter aims to take a concise journey through the vast mass of knowledge that science has revealed to humankind, particularly over the last few decades. A question of teleology must arise to any thinking individual—is there an engine that initiated and drives this universe, or is it just simply a "brute fact" and "that's that"?[7]

The Basic Building Blocks of the Universe —From Simplicity to Complexity

The Elementary Particles of Nature

The standard model of elementary particles describes the seventeen elementary particles which make up all matter in the universe.[8] It also details the four fundamental forces of nature responsible for the integrity of the universe, three of which—the electromagnetic force, the strong force, and the weak force—have been defined and characterized, while the fourth force, the gravitational force remains to be elucidated. Thus, the classical components of the atomic model, protons, neutrons, and electrons, have now been further dissected into elementary particles detected through high speed collision analyses in linear accelerators, such as the Large Hadron Collider in Geneva. These elementary particles are broadly subdivided into fermions—particles whose

---

6. Gribbin, *Schrodingers Kittens*.

7. Bertrand Russell is reputed to have retorted in a radio debate that "the Universe is a brute fact" and "the Universe just exists and that's that." "Fr. Copleston vs. Bertrand Russell."

8. Bevelacqua, "Standard Model of Particle Physics," 613–23. Hawking, *Brief History of Time*, 71.

quantum spin number is an odd multiple of 1/2, and bosons, or force particles, whose spin quantum number is zero, or an integral number. Fermions are then subdivided into quarks (up and down quarks) and leptons. Protons are made up of 2 up and 1 down quark, and neutrons are made up of 1 up and 2 down quarks. The leptons are comprised of the electrons, which are partially particle-like and partially wave-like, and the electron neutrino. Since the first description of these elementary particles of matter were described, two further generations of elementary particles have been described, making up the family of twelve fermions. In addition to the fermions, five bosons, or force particles, have been described related to the fundamental forces of nature.

Four fundamental forces determine how the universe is maintained, each associated with its own force particle/boson:

The Fundamental Forces of Nature.

1. The electromagnetic force, governing the attraction of unlike charges (+ve/-ve), or repulsion of like charges (+ve/+ve or -ve/-ve). The force particle for the electromagnetic force is the photon.

2. The strong force, which keeps the quarks together to form the proton and the neutron; the force particle is the gluon.

3. The weak force, far weaker than both electromagnetic and the strong force; it is responsible for radioactive decay. Three force particles are associated with the weak force, the W+, the W-, and the Z bosons.

4. The gravitational force. The fourth force, which is an extremely weak force for individual particles, is the gravitational force. Little is understood within today's frontier of knowledge regarding its force particle, and, in point of fact, in a quantum model in terms of elementary particles, gravity doesn't yet exist. This frontier of knowledge has yet to be reached.

The earlier simplistic concept of the atomic structure of matter described a nuclear proton and neutron, with an orbiting electron, much like the Earth orbiting around the sun in the solar system. This idea has been upended by modern particle physics and the standard model of elementary particles. Empty space, very much a part of the earlier concept of atomic structure, is not empty at all and is, in fact, filled with continuous background fields, including the Higgs field. It is the interaction of elementary particles with the Higgs field that imparts mass to matter, the responsible particle in Higgs field being the Higgs boson—detected in July 2012 in the Large Hadron Collider.[9]

Thus, the physics of the latter part of the second decade of the twenty-first century, understands the constitution of the universe on the standard model of elementary particles. In this model the entire universe, from an inanimate rock to the complexities of the living human brain to the farthest star in the universe, is comprised, simply, of those 17 elementary particles, held together by the 4 fundamental forces, within the continuous fields of the cosmos.

The Creation of Life

Evolution, and perhaps more specifically human evolution, occupies center stage in the science-religion dialogue. *The Origin of Species* by Charles Darwin, published in 1859, had a deep and profound effect on human society. After the Bible it was deemed to be the second most influential book, according to a 2014 United Kingdom poll conducted by the Folio Society.[10] Its profound influence on theology has been felt to this day. In the century-and-a-half since the publication of *Origin of Species* the science of evolutionary biology has developed into a gigantic scientific discipline, penetrating extensively into many branches of science and even into the practice of medicine (with the publication of several books and even a regular peer-reviewed journal on the subject of evolutionary medicine[11]). The evidence for evolution is unequivocally

---

9. ATLAS, "Combined Search," 49–66.

10. BBC, "Bible Tops 'Most Influential.'"

11. "The Journal of Evolutionary Medicine is a scholarly open access, peer-reviewed, and fully refereed journal. The goal of the journal is to improve

convincing to the overwhelming majority of scientists. Nevertheless a sizable proportion of the general population still rejects evolution, considering it to be a threat to their religious convictions. For example, a third of Americans polled in 2013 by a Pew Research analysis rejected the idea of evolution, ascribing rather to "humans and living things have existed in the present form since the beginning of time."[12] The "beginning of time" for 42 percent of Americans is the "biblical" 10,000 years ago.[13]

The origin and development of life can be considered in two stages—abiogenesis, the formation of living forms from non-living inorganic materials; and biogenesis, the development of living organisms from organic material into the species of animals and plants which cover the Earth's surface.

Abiogenesis

Abiogenesis is also referred to as prebiotic synthesis. One of the earliest hypotheses on the origin of life was proposed by the British scientist, J. B. S. Haldane (1892–1964), and also, in a book, *The Origin of Life*, published in 1936, by the Soviet biochemist, Aleksandr Oparin[14] (1894–1980). Realizing that the early atmosphere of the earth, over 4 billion years ago, was rich in methane gas, water, and ammonia, the Oparin-Haldane hypothesis put forward the idea that the mixing of these starting materials, and the addition of a source of energy, such as lightning or geothermal activity, could have synthesized organic materials from inorganic chemicals. In 1953, at the University of Chicago, the hypothesis was tested experimentally by Stanley Miller and Harold Urey.[15] They combined ammonia, methane, water vapor, and hydrogen in a flask to mimic the early Earth's atmosphere, and passed an electric

the understanding of medical issues through the integration of evolutionary principles and perspectives." Editorial policy of the journal, Ashdin Publishing.
   12. Pew Research, "Public Views on Human Evolution."
   13. Gallup, "42 percent Believe Creationist View."
   14. Oparin, *Origin of Life*.
   15. Miller and Urey, "Organic Compound Synthesis," 245–51.

current through the mixture to simulate lightning activity. Over twenty different amino acids (the building blocks of proteins) were produced. Since then numerous hypotheses on the origin of life in early Earth have been proposed. Some have conjectured that life may have even been brought to earth from extra-terrestrial sources—organic molecules have been demonstrated on Mars,[16] and even on comets.[17] The earliest evidence of life on Earth has been found in fossils in hydrothermal vent precipitates dating back to 3.8 to 4.3 billion years ago.[18] Despite the numerous hypotheses and associated experimental and observational studies, the origin of life on earth brings science to another frontier of knowledge, which remains to be explored.

Biogenesis—the Origin of Living Organisms

Unlike the somewhat enigmatic abiogenesis, the related biological discipline of biogenesis has been extensively studied with a vast storehouse of scientifically verifiable evidence. The science of biological evolution has been explained in a number of publications that are very palatable to the lay person.[19] Briefly, the process of evolution of species can be described as having two components:

1. Firstly, as a result of a genetic change an organism acquires some novel genetic coding for a trait or traits that give it a competitive advantage in the environment in which it finds itself. This change would be the result mainly of random mutations due to occasional imperfections in the DNA copying mechanism, and/or other processes for generating

---

16. Hand, "Mars Rover," 1402–3.
17. Capaccioni et al., "Organic-rich surface," 628-1–4.
18. Dodd et al., "Evidence for Early Life," 60–74.
19. Coyne, *Why Evolution is True*. Dawkins, *Greatest Show on Earth*. Miller, *Finding Darwin's God*. National Academy of Sciences, *Science, Evolution and Creationism*.

genetic diversity such as translocation[20] or transfection.[21] It is important to emphasize that, while mutations are random, the selective pressure for developing advantageous traits is non-random and directional—i.e., it is purposefully aimed towards ultimately improving the ability of the species to survive in order to reproduce.

2. The second component consolidates the hereditarily advantageous trait (or traits) by passing it on to succeeding generations. The selection of these traits is then maintained when the bearer is reproductively isolated by, for example, geographic isolation, or physical terrain barriers such as mountain ranges or deserts. This is analogous to the way animal breeders artificially select for pedigreed domestic animals. In the natural environment, a new species arises as a result of the reproductive isolation mechanism preventing interbreeding with related species. Animal breeders similarly follow the same process as in nature, by selecting specific, desirable traits in domestic animals, and isolating their breeding to those pedigrees possessing the desired trait or traits.

Evolution—Fact or Theory?

Much of the misunderstanding of evolution by the general public, especially those who follow a creationist standpoint, stems from a misunderstanding of the scientific usage of the term "theory." In scientific language, "theory" is used to connote a collection of facts established and validated by the rules of the scientific method, to explain particular phenomena—as discussed in the previous chapter. The theory of evolution thus shares the same degree of factual acceptance as the germ theory and the atomic theory. The validated scientific evidence supporting evolution is vast.

---

20. Translocation is the process of genetic material detaching itself and reinserting in a different location—sometimes referred to as "jumping genes."

21. Transfection is the introduction and integration of new genetic material into the organism by an infecting agent such as a virus.

An essential requirement for the biological process to evolve new species is time. The age of the earth, 4.5 billion years, has been established by several different technologies, including radiometric dating using the precision intrinsic to the decay time of radioactive isotopes (the foundation of the atomic clock—the most precise timekeeper of all). Data from all these different methods are in total agreement with each other.

Very briefly, the major scientific disciplines confirming the natural evolution of species, include the following:

1. **Paleontology**: I.e., the study of the fossil record. The criterion of falsifiability, required by the scientific method to validate any scientific research, could readily be applied to paleontological science, by finding fossils of more advanced life forms in earlier rock strata. In all of paleontological research this has never occurred—universally, fossil records of life forms have been found in rock strata corresponding precisely to the predicted vintage of the organism. A well-publicized example was the successful discovery of the transitional marine-land organism Tiktaalik ("large freshwater fish"), found in rock strata at precisely the predicted age of 550 million years ago.[22]

2. **Biogeography**: I.e., the study of the distribution of animals and plant life in different geographic locations. For example, the parallels between the marsupial species in Australia, isolated by vast stretch of ocean, which have evolved similarly but separately to analogous non-marsupial species in Eurasia and Africa. Another example of the clearly manifested characteristics of the evolutionary process is the very characteristic specific evolution of animal and plant species in isolated islands, such as the Galapagos archipelago.

3. **Rudimentary Non-functional Relics of Organs**: which were fully and indispensably functional in earlier forms of life, for example the human coccyx (tail) bone.

4. **Commonality of Biochemical and Genetic Mechanisms**: in all living forms—indicating a common ancestry.

22. Daeschler et al., "Devonian Tetrapod-like Fish," 757–63.

5. Molecular Genetics: The most powerful supporting evidence comes from molecular genetic studies and the homologies of nucleic acid sequences between related species.

The Theology of Evolution

> Darwin's theory is no more to do with philosophy than any other hypothesis in the natural sciences.[23]

More than any other scientific discipline, evolutionary biology is that science which is most often and most prominently featured in the science-religion debate. On the level of scientific veracity and faithfulness to the rules of the scientific method, evolutionary biology succeeds more than most scientific disciplines. However, as Wittgenstein has posited, and as biological scientists with religious faith have pondered, does evolution answer the deeper ontological questions around living organisms, and especially with respect to humans?

There is a clear dualistic approach to interpreting the factuality of the theory of evolution. Atheism hailed the advent of evolution theory as an indication that materialist philosophy embraced living organisms as well as the inanimate. As Richard Dawkins proclaimed: "Darwin has made it possible to be an intellectually fulfilled atheist."[24] However, there is a contrary and more profound interpretation of evolutionary theory—that the fundamentals of genetic modification and natural selection represent a powerful message of teleology, specifically, that of the underlying etiology of the biological drive. The import of the biological drive, in particular, the universality of both the sexual drive and the parenting drive throughout the animal kingdom, deserves a deeper interpretation than merely the reductive reasoning of materialism. Deeper reflection, beyond that limited to an empirical analysis of scientific findings, needs to take into account the extent and the universality of the biological drives. The power of the sexual drive and the parenting

---

23. Wittgenstein, *Tractatus Logico-Philosophicus*, 30.
24. Dawkins, *Blind Watchmaker*, 6.

drive which, on occasion, even exceeds that of individual survival, in order to preserve and improve the species, would appear to point to a teleology which underpins evolution. The science of biological evolution in the modern era, rather than being the fundament of non-belief, has much to support it being a potent buttress for the teleological proof of the existence of God.

Cosmology—Towards its Knowledge Frontier

As the nineteenth century advanced into the twentieth century, astronomers gazing at the sky through optical telescopes were reasonably satisfied with a static universe made up of a solar system of eight planets, the constellations of stars and the Milky Way. Absolute time and absolute space were governed largely by Newtonian physics and mechanics. The twentieth century saw the birth of the new sciences of cosmology and astrophysics, which radically changed our knowledge of the universe we live in. Revolutionary ideas such as Einstein's theories of general and special relativity, combined with powerful instrumentation such as the Large Hadron Collider, radio and x-ray astronomy, and the Hubble space telescope, have unlocked a universe of unimaginable proportions.

The concept of a static universe, supported by Einstein at the turn of the century, was first questioned in 1912 by the discoveries of the American astronomer, Vesto Slipher (1876–1969). Using spectroscopic analysis, he described the red shift of galaxies, which indicated that the universe was not static but was expanding at an enormous rate.[25] This red shift-distance correlation later became known as Hubble's law and formed the modern model of the expanding universe. The Belgian Catholic priest, George Lemaitre (1894–1966) confirmed Slipher's red shift-based descriptions of the expanding universe.[26] In 1931 Lemaitre went on to trace cosmic events back in time, to put forward the epochal proposal that the universe began with a single quantum, which the British

25. Slipher, "Nebulae," 403–9.
26. Lemaitre, "Evolution of the Expanding Universe," 12–17.

astronomer Fred Hoyle jocularly (in a radio interview) termed the "Big Bang." In 1929 the American astronomer Edwin Hubble (1889–1953) showed that the greater the distance of the galaxy, the faster it was expanding—Hubble's law.[27] One of the most significant advances in cosmology came in May 1964 with the incidental discovery of the cosmic microwave background (CMB, also known as the cosmic background radiation), by two American physics Nobel Laureates, Arno Penzias (1933–) and Robert Wilson (1936–).[28] Noticing a low-level background "hiss" in their radio telescope antenna, they went on to show it to be due to the cosmic radiation remnants of electromagnetic radiation produced during the early stages of the birth of the universe, following soon after the Big Bang. Studies from the Cosmic Background Explorer (COBE, a satellite dedicated to CMB studies), as well as experimental evidence from the giant particle collider, have provided a detailed history of the universe.[29]

The History of the Universe[30]

The universe is understood to have begun some 13.8 billion years ago with what is referred to as the singularity—a one-dimensional point of infinite density and heat, where the laws of physics cease to operate. In the first 10^{-43} seconds of the universe, the heat was so intense that atomic structure was shattered and matter existed only as subatomic particles, quarks, and electrons. All four of the fundamental forces were fused into a super force. In the next second, the universe had cooled sufficiently for the four forces to separate, and the first subatomic particles were able to hold together. Further cooling at three minutes of age stabilized subatomic particles so that by seventeen minutes, atoms were formed. The temperature was high enough for nuclear fusion to take place and hydrogen,

27. Kragh and Smith, "Expanding Universe," 141–62.
28. Wilson, "Cosmic Microwave Background Radiation," 433–49.
29. See Smoot, "Cosmic Background Explorer," 136–47.
30. Turner, "Origin of the Universe," 36–43.

deuterium, helium, and some lithium had formed. At 20 minutes, the primordial ratio of hydrogen to helium, 3:1, mimicked the constitution of the sun (75 percent hydrogen: 25 percent helium). Structures started to form as gravity began to overcome the enormous heat, leading to the formation of the galaxies. At this point electrons were unable to bond with atomic nuclei and the universe was ionized. At 380,000 years the universe had cooled sufficiently for electrons to combine with atomic nuclei to form stable neutral atoms for the first time—a process termed recombination. An important modification to this narrative of the evolution of the universe is the so-called inflationary universe theory put forward in 1981 by the American physicist Alan Guth (1947–),[31] and confirmed by numerous experiments over the past 20 to 30 years. It proposes that cosmic inflation occurred extremely rapidly, almost immediately after the Big Bang. In other words, at between 10^{-36} to 10^{-32} seconds the universe increased in size by a factor of 10^{26}. These events have been recorded from photons emitted during the tumultuous early life of the universe. These photons red-shifted to the microwave band, and are detected today as the cosmic microwave background. At 400 million years after the Big Bang, normal matter collected, and the first stars formed becoming the galaxies and the clusters of galaxies of today.

Our Universe

To the trained cosmologist, the dimensions of the universe are true, scientifically verifiable and palpably real. To anyone outside of the science, these distances are beyond comprehension. The conventional astronomical unit (AU) of distance is defined as the average distance between the sun and the earth, about 93 million miles (150 million km). While this unit is useful for measurements within the solar system, it has become more common usage to measure astronomical distances in light years. The universal physical constant for the speed of light in a vacuum, developed

31. Guth, *Inflationary Universe*.

from Einstein's special relativity, is 300,000 km/s (186,000 miles/s). (There have been some suggestions that there may be some variability to this constant).[32] A light year is thus the distance traveled by light in a year. To put it into a more everyday perspective, the light we perceive from the sun is light that left the sun some eight minutes previously. The nearest star to earth (other than the sun), is the triple star Alpha Centauri, which is 4.3 light-years away. Our galaxy, the Milky Way, is a spiral galaxy consisting of several billion stars and is 100 000 light-years in diameter. The closest spiral galaxy to earth, which is also the most distant object visible to the naked eye, is Andromeda, some 2.5 million light-years away. The light we perceive from Andromeda left that galaxy when the first precursors of *Homo sapiens*, the Australopithecines, walked the earth. Clearly, space travel beyond our solar system with current chemically-propelled spacecraft, which travel at only 1/40,000 the speed of light, will have to remain in the realm of science fiction. Furthermore, as the universe is calculated to be 13.8 billion years old, that sets the limit to what can ever be known of the universe—i.e., a distance of 13.8 billion light-years away. However, because of the expansion of the universe, the observable universe limit, also known as the cosmic horizon, is estimated at 42 billion light-years away. Beyond that horizon the universe is, by definition, totally hidden from humankind. Peering into the "emptiest" part of the universe, the so-called Hubble Deep Field, it is estimated that there are well over 100 billion galaxies each containing billions of stars.[33] Standing out amongst the galaxies are the most luminous objects, the quasars. For example, the quasar 3C273 blasts out an energy over four trillion times the energy of our sun and has a core temperature of over ten trillion °C.[34] However, being 2.5 billion light-years away, it appears as a faint object.

32. Barrow, "Cosmologies," 043515–22.

33. Sparke and Gallagher, *Galaxies in the Universe*. Sutter, *Your Place in the Universe*.

34. Courvoisier and Robson, "Quasar 3C273," 50–57.

Stars, including our sun, have life cycles of birth and death as their thermonuclear generators run down.[35] Higher mass stars exhaust their energy more rapidly than lower mass stars. Our sun is estimated to have a lifespan of 12 billion years and has about 7 billion years left. Stars less than 1.5 times the mass of the sun become white dwarfs, which are extremely dense, one mL having a mass of a metric ton. They are also extremely hot, reaching temperatures exceeding 100,000°C. Larger stars, up to 2.8 times the mass of the sun, collapse to become neutron stars with even denser bodies—one mL having a mass of 400 million tons. With the supermassive stars, which have a mass over 2.8 times the mass of the sun, the gravitational force is so great that nothing is able to escape, even light, resulting in an invisible, infinitely deep hole, the Black Hole. Supermassive black holes of up to millions of solar masses exist in the center of nearly all large galaxies, including our own galaxy the Milky Way, and probably provided the gravitational force which held the galaxy together during its formation.

Amongst the most unusual and poorly understood phenomena of the universe are dark matter and dark energy. Work by the American astronomer Vera Rubin (1928–2016) has demonstrated that up to 90 percent of matter in the universe is not visible, i.e., is dark matter.[36] Its existence is derived from studies of the orbits of stars and clouds of gas in the centers of spiral galaxies where it was observed that they moved too fast to be accounted for by the gravitational pull of the visible matter of the galaxies (sometimes referred to as the "galactic rotational problem"). What dark matter is, is still not known—perhaps it is some mysterious subatomic particles which have never been detected. Equally enigmatic is dark energy, an unknown energy which is thought to permeate space.[37] Space, therefore, does not appear to be "empty" but is, in fact, suffused with energy. Dark energy is postulated to be the responsible force for balancing the expansion of the universe with the counteracting gravitational force, which contracts the

35. Hawking, *Brief History of Time*, 91.
36. Rubin, "Dark Matter," 106–10.
37. Copeland et al., "Dynamics of Dark Energy," 1753–1935.

universe. The known universe, i.e., the universe that is observed, characterized, studied, and described, thus comprises only about 5 percent of the total universe—27 percent is dark matter and 68 percent is dark energy.

What Do We Understand of the Universe?

To what extent has science brought humankind to grasping the depth of understanding of our world? Much of the mysteries of the quantum world still defy explanations. The wave-particle duality has revised the classical concept of a particle, and demonstrates that all particles can be partly described as waves. Similarly, electromagnetic waves, such as light, behave to some extent as a stream of particulate matter. The classical double slit experiment, originally performed in the early 1800s, demonstrates the wave-like behavior of light by passing it through two slits next to each other, showing that waves interfere or amplify each other. Particles, such as electrons, passed through the double slits similarly demonstrate wave-like behavior. Strangely, however, the pattern disappears when a detector is used to determine which slit the particle goes through, i.e., apparently when "notice" is taken, and reappears when the detector is removed before the particles hit the screen.[38] Another unexplained quantum phenomenon is the concept of quantum entanglement, which describes the attachment between two objects with complementarity of their spin orientation, even if the two objects are separated from each other by vast distances.[39] Perhaps the most famous thought experiment in physics is that of the cat-in-the-box, devised in 1935 by the quantum physicist Erwin Schrodinger (1887–1961).[40] It describes a paradox in quantum physics of the uncertain predicament of a theoretical cat in a box that could be both dead and alive until the box is opened and the status of the cat is determined. Modern theoretical

38. Anathaswamy, *Through Two Doors at Once*.
39. Horodecki et al., "Quantum Entanglement," 865–942.
40. Castelvecchi, "Quantum Puzzle Baffles Physicists," 446–47.

physics has defined numerous other enigmatic phenomena such as antimatter,[41] string theory,[42] and others, illustrating the very embryonic stage of the understanding and the measurement of the reality of the physical world at the present time. What lies ahead of the knowledge frontier is vast. Future scientists will move that knowledge frontier greatly forward to elucidate the scientific enigmas of today. However, following the Sisyphean pattern of science, these answers will give birth to many more mysteries and enigmas. The complexity of the universe is clearly well beyond human understanding, and will continue to defy human attempts to describe their purpose in physical terms.

The Fine-tuning of the Universe and the Anthropic Principle

It is well to end this chapter on two related subjects that really are the pinnacle of the modern teleological argument. These are the fine-tuning of the universe for life, and the fine-tuning for human life, the anthropic principle. On reviewing the physical and mathematical laws that governed the evolution of the universe and which sustain its continued existence, it is apparent that these forces are exquisitely balanced on a knife-edge of parameters. Had there been even slight deviation from these values, the universe as we know it would not exist. Not surprisingly the fine-tuning argument and the anthropic principle have been of great interest not only to scientists, but also to philosophers and theologians.

The Fine-tuning of the Universe—the Six Numbers

Sir Martin Rees (1942–), the Astronomer Royal, has famously summarized these fine-tuning parameters into six independent numbers[43]:

41. Dine and Kusenko, "Matter-Antimatter Asymmetry," 1–30.
42. Wray, *Introduction to String Theory*.
43. Rees, *Just Six Numbers*.

1. **Omega.** This number relates to the mass of the universe including the galaxies, dark matter, and gas clouds. The number denotes the ratio between the gravitational force, which is dependent on the total mass of the universe, and the expansion energy of the universe. Gravity would contract the universe and, if unopposed by the expansion energy, would collapse it into what is referred to as "the Big Crunch." If the gravitational force is too weak, matter would fly apart and be unable to form galaxies. The *omega* number = one, but the exact number and the tolerance in either side still needs to be calculated.[44]

2. **Epsilon.** This is a measure of the strong force (one of the four fundamental forces of nature mentioned above) which binds the subatomic constituents together, and is responsible for the process of nuclear fusion which converts the hydrogen atom to helium, and then on to the heavier elements. The *epsilon* number is 0.007 and any deviation from this value on either side would mean we could not exist. If it was 0.006 or less, the strong force would be insufficient for fusion to heavier elements from hydrogen. If it was 0.008 or more, rapid fusion of hydrogen would soon mop up all the hydrogen and leave the universe devoid of fuel and water.

3. **N.** N is a measure of the balance between the electromagnetic force in the atom and the vastly weaker gravitational force. The value of N is 10^{36}. Change of this value, for example to 10^{30}, would be inimical to life.

4. **Q.** Q represents the energies that existed after the Big Bang when the universe expanded, resulting in areas of more dense and less dense material. In time these clusters of matter went on to form the galaxies and stars, which were held together by gravity. The strength of the forces needed to maintain the

---

44. The famed British astrophysicist Stephen Hawking has expressed the tolerance of the ratio of gravitational force to the expansion of the universe immediately after the Big Bang, as "If the rate of expansion one second after the Big Bang had been smaller by even one part in a hundred thousand million million, it would have re-collapsed before it reached its present size." Hawking, *Brief History of Time*, 138.

clustering is measured by the strength of the energy required to break them up. Q is estimated to be 10^{-5}. If smaller, the universe would be inert and without structure. If larger, it would be dominated by giant black holes.

5. **Lambda.** This is the number developed from the accelerated expansion of the universe and is controlled by a novel cosmic "antigravity." Its value is approximately 0.7. A larger *lambda* would cause the universe to expand too rapidly for galaxies, planets, and stars to form, and a smaller *lambda* would mean a slowdown in the expansion of the universe, and distortion in the formation of the planets, galaxies, and stars, which would be unable to support life.

6. **D.** D is the number of spatio-temporal dimensions. We are familiar with four dimensions, three of space and one of time. A consequence of a three-dimensional spatial world is that forces such as gravity operate in an inverse square law—the force from a mass or a charge at twice the distance is four times weaker. The stability of the planetary orbits in the solar system would be lost if gravity operated as an inverse cube (four spatial dimensions) or inverse square (two spatial dimensions).

The Anthropic Principle

The anthropic principle is something that dwells more in the spheres of philosophy and theology than in science. As discussed above, scientists have produced data documenting exquisitely sensitive numbers on which the universe depends. In addition to these cosmological parameters, several other "Goldilocks" properties of the universe are similarly precisely poised for sentient life. For example, the universe is old enough for nucleosynthesis by fusion to have taken place in the furnaces of stars to form elements beyond hydrogen, helium, and lithium. (Based on this understanding our bodies and those of all living organisms are formed, in part, from stellar dust.) However, it is not too old for stellar energy sources to have degraded. The planet Earth is also ideally situated in the solar system for suitable temperatures for water to be liquid. Another example is the availability of the element carbon with its four valence covalent bonds, which make it an ideal element to allow for the production of long-chain molecules, which are the building blocks of living organisms. Many other "Goldilocks" examples have been recognized.[45] Interpretation of these scientific revelations has, not surprisingly, been controversial, with theists proposing purpose and nonbelievers defending fortunate random occurrence. The word "anthropic" relates specifically to humans, although the principle itself is broader and defines conditions supporting the existence of the universe and all its properties as we know it.

The weak anthropic principle, first described by Brandon Carter in 1973, views the fortuity of the fine-tuning of the universe as simply because there happens to be an observer who is describing them—us.[46] In other words, these conditions are there merely because of an observer being there to quantify and describe them. The strong anthropic principle of John Barrow and Frank Tippler, which is less accepted in the scientific world, asserts that the properties of the universe make it inevitable that intelligent life would develop.[47] The debates around purpose, design, accident, and coincidence are numerous. Essentially these numbers represent a highly complex universe that is exquisitely sensitive to their constancy. How are these scientific data interpreted? Essentially there are three possible interpretations:

1. **The multiverse response:** This has been favored by much of the scientific community. It proposes that the universe we live in is just one of many millions, if not billions or even an infinite number, of universes, with countless permutations of physical properties. Our universe is simply the one where all the parameters happen to have come together to

---

45. Corey, *God Hypothesis*. Davies, *Goldilocks Enigma*.
46. Carter, "Large Number Coincidences," 291–98.
47. Barrow, *Anthropic Cosmological Principle*.

facilitate life. The multiverse hypothesis has been challenged by the South African cosmologist, George Ellis (1939–), citing a lack of scientific evidence to support this speculation.[48] It also runs counter to the principle of Occam's razor.[49] In a later article Ellis and Silk criticize the multiverse hypothesis as undermining science by advancing speculative theories of the universe which avoid experimental verification.[50] As contemporary philosopher Richard Swinburne has pointed out, it is simply vastly more probable that God created our universe conducive to life than that there is an almost infinitely large multiverse not created by God.[51] (A variation of the multiverse hypothesis postulates the existence of a hypervariable mega-universe, which suggests that pocket universes or bubble universes within the universe may provide life-sustaining conditions.[52]) The fundamental weakness of the multiverse hypothesis is that it remains unprovable because knowledge is limited by the speed of light (and all electromagnetic radiation)—as mentioned above. What lies beyond 42 billion light-years away, cannot, by definition, ever be known—it is the ultimate cosmic horizon.

2. **Future science:** Although the multiverse and other speculations are not presently founded on verifiable science, future scientists may well provide naturalistic explanations for fine-tuning. A weakness to this argument is the very nature of science itself—the Sisyphean cycle of science. While future science may well explain the current enigmas, future science could, as well, create at least as many, if not more, enigmas in

48. Ellis, "Does the Multiverse Really Exist," 38–43.

49. Also known as Ockham's razor or Ocham's Razor after the English Franciscan Friar William of Ockham (c. 1287–1347) who is credited with the idea. It is sometimes referred to as the Law of Parsimony and is a principle which applies to problem-solving when competing reasons are given for a specific problem. The principle states that the simplest and most direct explanation is the correct one.

50. Ellis and Silk, "Defend the Integrity of Physics," 321–23.

51. Swinburne, *Is There a God*, 58–62.

52. Walsh, "Ideology in Physics," 1–17.

the future—as scientific history has so amply demonstrated to date.

3. **Purposeful creation by the Creator:** This is the argument of the theist. It remains the simplest, most direct, explanation, which is not reliant on randomness, probability, or extrapolations to infinity, and satisfies Occam's Razor. If science remains the arbiter of truth, this argument does not produce the necessary scientific evidence. However, the evidence which is needed will come not from science but from revelation and reason.

4

The Human Organism and the Human Soul

> When I behold Your heavens, the work of Your fingers, the moon and stars that You set in place, what is man that You have been mindful of him, mortal man that You have taken note of him, that You have made him little less than divine and adorned him with glory and majesty; You have made him master over Your handiwork, laying the world at his feet.
>
> —Ps 8:4–7

The Changing Anthropic Paradigm

IN 1610, THE ITALIAN astronomer Galileo Galilei (1564–1642) published his *Sidereus Nuncius* (Starry Messenger), confirming the heliocentric solar system which Nicolaus Copernicus had earlier put forward in 1543, *De Revolutionibus Orbium Coelestium*.[1] This signature event marked the beginning of the upending of religious dogma by modern science. The geocentric view of the universe with the Earth, the domicile of humankind, at its center, as proposed by Aristotle and Ptolemy, had been the accepted position of the church, which also complied with the scriptural prescript of the centrality of humankind. Tried by the Inquisition in 1616 and again in 1633, Galileo was found guilty of heresy against religion and forced under threat of torture to recant. He was sentenced to

1. Finocchiaro, *Galileo*.

live the last nine years of his life under house arrest. Only in 1992 was he finally pardoned and vindicated by Pope John Paul II.

Some two and a half centuries after Galileo in 1859, a second seismic challenge to religious dogma took place with the publication of the book *On the Origin of Species* by the British naturalist Charles Darwin.[2] The book became an instant bestseller and is probably still one of the most influential books ever written. Its demonstration that life evolved by selection, rather than by design, threw it headlong into conflict with the literal interpretation of biblical creation. As mentioned in earlier chapters, significant proportions of the American population today still cling to the conservative religious dogma of the special creation of animal species and, in particular, the uniqueness of the creation of humans.

Thus did the birth of cosmology and biology launch the science assault on religious scriptural dogma—still very much alive today. A central theme of modern science has been the dethroning of the unique creation, and the special centrality, of humankind according to literal biblical narrative. Advancing scientific knowledge has served to provide even more evidence to further that challenge. However, the advance of modern science can also be interpreted that it may now well be bringing us full circle back to the specialness of humans. Could the most modern scientific advances provide evidence to support a universe created for humans, as discussed in the previous chapter, under the anthropic principle? Does the inability of advanced neurosciences to demonstrate apparent non-material constituents of the human organism, perhaps indicate the specialness of the human creation? Is the human being a special and unique creation in the universe? Religion would certainly have us believe this. References in the holy Scriptures state this unequivocally. On the sixth day of creation, humans were created in the image of God (Gen 1:27), and the soul of the human came from the Almighty breathing the breath of life into his nostrils (Gen 2:7). Humans were given dominion over all the animals of the world (Gen 1:26, 28). Human specialness is emphasized in many religious writings, e.g., Ps 115:16: "The heavens

2. Darwin, *Origin of Species*.

belong to the Lord but the earth He gave over to man." The Talmud[3] confirms the centrality of humans in a negative way through the narrative of the flood, where God "vindicates" the destruction of "innocent" animals as they serve no purpose if humankind was being destroyed. How does the theological concept of human specialness align with today's scientific scrutiny?

The Biological Human Organism

Within the evolutionary timescale of living organisms, the human species is but a tiny speck tacked onto the very end of a long procession of events. Thus, representing the history of the earth as an imaginary 24-hour time clock, life would arrive at 4:00 a.m., single-celled algae at 2:08 p.m., dinosaurs at 10:56 p.m., mammals at 11:39 p.m., while humans would have made their appearance at 43 seconds before midnight. And yet, it is the human species that has been solely responsible for some of the most dramatic changes to planet Earth. The impact of humans on the Earth's atmosphere, ecosystems, biosphere, geology, hydrology, and climate, has been so far-reaching that it has been proposed that the most recent epoch of geological age, since humans inhabited the planet, be designated the Anthropocene geologic time period.[4] The Anthropocene has been variously dated from as early as the agricultural revolution of 12,000 to 15,000 years ago, or the industrial revolution of 1862, or as recent as mid-1945, when the first nuclear weapon was detonated. Inarguably, the human species, by virtue of the impact it has made on the planet and on all other living organisms, occupies a unique position radically different from any other living being. The dominance of the human species is clearly not due to any of its physical properties or physical capabilities—many animals are stronger, faster, and have more sensitive sensory organs. Humans are also not unique amongst animals with respect to memory and emotion—many mammalian species also possess

---

3. b. Sanhedrin 108a.
4. Steffen et al., "Anthropocene," 614–21.

these properties.[5] The faculty of intelligence itself is not unique to humans—mammals and birds do exhibit intelligent planning behavior to the extent of tool-making, as seen in subhuman primates and certain birds,[6] even though there is a vast quantitative difference. Similarly with communication, many animals including invertebrates are able to communicate with each other; however there is no evidence of the development of language in any animal other than humans.[7]

Not surprisingly, therefore, the evolutionary history of humankind has been studied far more extensively than any other living species. Paleontological evidence suggests that the first hominins,[8] i.e., the lineage of human progenitors, diverged from the ancestral lineage of the chimpanzees and the apes approximately seven million years ago, with the advent of *Sahelanthropus tchadensis*—the earliest discovered hominin.[9] Climate change immediately preceding this period of time caused the forests of Africa to recede and be replaced by the typical open savanna landscape of southern and eastern Africa of today. A critical hominin adaptation, that of bipedalism, while it may have originated in the forest canopy to facilitate climbing and locomotion in the forest, later became a major selective advantage for life on the ground in the savanna. As early as 1871, Charles Darwin had hypothesized the selective advantage of bipedalism in the evolution of humans; for example, the freeing of the hands for making and using tools and weapons, for food gathering, and for self-defense.[10] Since then a variety of selective benefits to bipedalism

---

5. Mendl et al., "Integrative and Functional," 2895–2904.
6. Armant and Horton, "Revisiting," 1199–1208.
7. Endler, "Animal Communication Systems," 215–25.
8. Hominids are primate members of the family *Hominidae*, which comprises the great apes, orangutans, gorillas, chimpanzees, and hominins. Hominins comprise humans and their extinct ancestral predecessors.
9. Gibbons, "Turning Back the Clock," 189–91. Roberts, *Evolution*, 62–63. Wood and Harrison, "Evolutionary Context," 347–52.
10. Darwin, *Descent of Man*, 144.

have been hypothesized.[11] The legacy of bipedalism has, however, unfortunately also left its mark in the myriad of musculoskeletal and other ailments, from low back pain to hemorrhoids, so commonly experienced by humans.[12]

The most important consequence of bipedalism in the hominin lineage, which ultimately led to *Homo sapiens*, was encephalization—the evolutionary increase in size and complexity of the brain. The brain size of *Australopithecus*, at approximately 400 to 600 mL, was equivalent to that of the modern chimpanzee. *Homo habilis* (800 mL) was the first effective tool-maker; followed by *Homo erectus* (900 mL), who became the earliest user of fire and the first to cook food; followed later by the arrival of the *Neanderthals*, who fashioned clothes and had a brain size equivalent to that of humans (approximately 1200 mL). *Pari passu* with the increase of brain size came, not only the development of useful skills such as tool-making, weaponry, and fire for warmth, protection, and cooking, etc., but also the progressive development of social and cultural characteristics.[13] Precisely what factors brought about this brain expansion remains a matter of speculation. The most prevalent opinion is the expensive-tissue hypothesis.[14] In terms of its demands for metabolic energy, the brain is the most demanding of all organs. The human brain, which is only 2 percent of body weight, consumes on average 20 percent of the body's energy budget.[15] Bipedalism freed up the upper limbs, which developed high mobility to make tools and throw weapons. As a result prey became more easily available and, in addition, the advent of fire and cooking made meat more palatable and digestible. The high protein and lipid diet, which is more energy-efficient, could possibly have been the fuel that fed the expanding brain. It remains an attractive hypothesis, although more recent studies have

---

11. Niemitz, "Evolution of the Upright Position," 241–63.
12. Pennisi, "Burden of a Being a Biped," 974.
13. Falk, "Evolution of Brain and Culture," 99–111.
14. Aiello and Wheeler, "Expensive Tissue Hypothesis," 199–221.
15. Herculano-Houzel, "Human Brain," 10661–68.

questioned the expensive-tissue hypothesis.[16] Paleoanthropology and neuroscience have collectively generated a vast knowledge of the development and the functioning of the human brain. How does this knowledge assist in the further understanding of the human mind? Is there a non-physical component of the human brain, perhaps unique to humans, which is beyond elucidation by science?

The Human Brain

Anyone who has had the experience of handling the 1.5 kg gelatinous pale organ called the human brain must experience some sense of wonderment that therein lay the memories, the emotions, the consciousness, and the experiences and personality of a human being. Within that organ are some hundred billion neurons (nerve cells), and perhaps ten to fifty-fold more glial cells (non-neural supporting cells).[17] Clearly, the cognitive brain functions, i.e., the combination of intellectual functions, thinking, understanding, learning, innovating, and imagining, are at a level vastly greater than that of any other animal. The famous naturalist Sir Richard Owen (1804–1892), the foremost opponent of Darwinian evolution of the time, supported his opposition to evolution by the argument that the human brain was an outlier amongst mammalian brains.[18] Thomas H. Huxley (1825–1895), known as "Darwin's bulldog," countered that human brains resemble those of the other apes in all fundamental aspects.

Neuroanatomists have long puzzled over the apparent similarity between human and mammalian brains. Paleontological studies have shown an obvious progressive evolutionary increase in size of hominin brains leading up to the human brain. Thus, the ratio of brain size to body mass ranges from 1.2 percent for *Australopithecus afarensis*, to 1.58 percent for *Homo habilis*, and from

---

16. Navarrete et al., "Energetics and Evolution," 91–93.
17. Herculano-Houzel, "Human Brain," 10661–68.
18. Striedter et al., "Brain and Behaviour," 10607–11.

1.98 percent for *Homo neanderthalensis* to 2.75 percent for *Homo sapiens*.[19] Size of brain is, however, in itself not a distinguishing feature of the human brain. The human brain is two to threefold smaller than the elephant brain, and four to sixfold smaller than that of the whale.[20] Could the cerebral cortex, the seat of cognition in the mammalian brain, provide any clue to the understanding of the advanced cognitive functions of the human brain? Although the human cerebral cortex is indeed the largest amongst mammals—from 75.5 percent to 84 percent of the total brain mass—other mammalian species are not far behind—73 percent for the chimpanzee and 74.5 percent for the horse. Similarly the number of neurons and non-neural cells is similar to other primates, as is the conductivity of the neurons as measured by the total number of synapses (neural connections).

In 2013 the BRAIN (Brain Research through Advancing Innovative New technologies) initiative was launched in the US to develop and to apply the most advanced new technologies to improve understanding of the human brain. Specifically, it will investigate the biological basis for its exceptional cognitive functionality.[21] The human brain is undoubtedly the most complex biological entity in the known universe. A true understanding of its workings is a frontier well beyond current science.

The Human Mind

The enormity of the biomedical sciences, and the extent of its practical applications in preventive and curative medicine, is testimony to the depth of knowledge and understanding achieved by the human organism. As with the other biomedical sciences, the neurosciences have made vast inroads into our understanding of the physiology of the brain. Advanced technologies, such as functional magnetic resonance imaging (fMRI), have anatomically

19. Roberts, *Evolution*, 32.
20. Herculano-Houzel, "Human Brain," 10661–68.
21. Jorgenson et al., "BRAIN Initiative," 1–12.

mapped the various functional components of the brain, including those parts of the brain responsible for mood, emotions, thought, and language.[22] However, the materiality of the human mind remains outside the purview of physical scientific exploration. A discussion of the complexities of the relationship between mental states and the physical world is beyond the scope of this volume. Keith Maslin has written an excellent introduction to the philosophy of mind.[23] Briefly, Maslin describes five major theories of the mind-body relation:

1. The Dualist Theory

One the first theories of the mind was the dualist theory, dating back to the ancient Greeks, but generally ascribed to René Descartes (1596–1650), and hence often referred to as Cartesian dualism.[24] According to Descartes, mental states can never be explained by the machinery of the brain, and thus the non-physical entity, the soul, is a separate entity attached to the body during life, but separated from it after death.

2. The Mind/Body Identity Theory

In contrast to Cartesian dualism, the strictly materialist viewpoint states that mental states are not separable from the physical, i.e., the mind and the body are the same.

3. Logical or Analytical Behaviorism.

This approach depicts the mind as being neither a physical nor an immaterial entity. Rather, it is a product of the pattern of actual and possible behavior.

---

22. Frackowiak, *Human Brain Function*.
23. Maslin, *Introduction*.
24. Hatfield, "Rene Descartes."

4. Functionalism

This also states that the mind is neither physical nor mental, but is a function of a program run on the hardware of the brain, which computes input from the senses.

5. Non-reductive Monism

This also rejects dualism in favor of a monistic, materialist standpoint, in which the mind integrates the inputs of theories 2, 3, and 4 but needs to explain the existence of consciousness as a feature of reality.

As it has been difficult to ascribe materiality to the mind, so is the definition of the mind suitably vague. Incorporating into what is understood to be the "mind" are brain functions of cognition, perception, consciousness, thinking, judgment, language, and memory. The mind also outputs as the individualistic personality—how a person is perceived in relation to his or her behavior, responses, outlook, and similar qualities, i.e., functions generally accepted to be governed by the mind.

The strictly materialist view of the mind would point out that profound changes in the mind can be caused by purely physical agents, such as mind-altering drugs, brain trauma, disease, and age or maturity of the brain. One of the most dramatic demonstrations of the effect of physical damage to the brain resulting in a radical change of personality is the celebrated neuroscience case study of the unfortunate Phineas Gage.[25] In 1848, Gage, a 25-year-old affable well-liked foreman at a railway construction site, suffered a horrendous injury. As a result of an explosion on the construction site, a tamping iron (used to compress explosives in rocks), 43 inches long, 1.25 inches in diameter, and weighing 13.25 pounds, shot off like a missile, entered Gage's left cheek under his eye and was propelled clean through his left cerebral cortex, landing eighty feet away covered in blood and brain tissue. Miraculously,

25. Van Horn et al., "Mapping Connectivity Damage," 1–24.

he survived and lived another twelve years. However, as a result of the injury he was "no longer Gage"—he became a belligerent, unpleasant individual, uttering profanities, i.e., an individual with a totally different mind.

Several arguments have been posited to counter the physicalist/materialist view of the mind. The advent of artificial intelligence has been argued by some to be a substitute for human brain intelligence—for example, to make doctors obsolete.[26] The Turing test, developed in 1950 by the brilliant English mathematician Alan Turing (1912–1954), is designed to assess whether a machine is able to emulate the intelligence of a human and "think" like a human being. It is designed to assess its ability to develop language to converse with a human.[27] No such machine learning, to this level, has yet been achieved.[28] Rather, it has been shown by the American philosopher, John Searle (1932–) that a computer program is unable, on its own, to substitute for mental processes, as the computer program is defined purely syntactically through symbol manipulation, unlike mental processes which require content.[29] Searle devised a famous thought experiment called the Chinese room experiment to illustrate that syntax alone is insufficient to produce meaningful semantic content. The thought experiment conceives of an individual receiving written questions in Chinese from Chinese-speaking participants in another room. A translating reference code book is provided to the individual with a means to respond with the correct answers. Nevertheless it is apparent that he/she would still not understand Chinese.

Another thought experiment, called Mary's room, was devised by Frank Jackson to support the knowledge argument against physicalism.[30] In this scenario, Mary, a specialist vision neurophysiologist, is confined in a black-and-white room with only a black-and-white TV monitor. Her life experiences have

---

26. Goldhahn et al., "Artificial Intelligence," 1–3.
27. Turing, "Computing Machinery and Intelligence," 433–60.
28. Warwick and Shoch, "Passing the Turing Test," 409–19.
29. Searle, "Theory of Mind," 10343–48.
30. Jackson, "What Mary Didn't Know," 291–95.

been purely black and white and without color. After leaving the room she is shown a red tomato. From this thought experiment the question is posed—does the redness represent new information to Mary that she is now acquiring beyond the physical dimensions of what "red" meant to her previously, from her purely materialistic scientific knowledge?[31] This knowledge or epiphenomenon of "redness," is referred to as qualia, and is deemed to be a property apart from the physical properties of the object, but resides in the consciousness of the perceiving individual. The physicalist/non-physicalist argument remains controversial, and indeed Jackson himself later rejected his own knowledge argument in favor of a physicalist belief.

The Human Soul

Related to the mind is the soul. In the religious sphere the soul is the non-material or spiritual identity of the individual that is attached to the material body, but is a separate entity. According to the religious view, the soul detaches from the body after death and, being non-material, is immortal.

The existence of a non-physical epiphenomenon of human consciousness is one which is in the realm of philosophical exploration, and may well be outside that of scientific investigation. The issue is one which is clearly of crucial theological relevance in relation to the entity of the human soul. The Cartesian duelist theory of the mind-body relationship aligns most closely with the existential question of the soul—the prime spiritual concept of individuality, distinct from the physical body. References to the existence of the soul abound in the holy Scriptures—from the creation of humans, Gen 2:7, through to Ps 104 ("bless my soul"). Even the transitory suspension of consciousness during sleep is, in the Orthodox Jewish faith, deemed to be a temporary detachment of the soul from the body—sleep is referred to as 1/60th of

---

31. Alter, "Knowledge Argument."

death in the Talmud.[32] There is, in fact, a special prayer of thanks to the Almighty for restoring one's soul on awakening from sleep, which forms part of the daily morning prayer.[33] The soul, in the religious world, is the essence of the individual, non-physical and not bound by space or any particular position in space.[34] It is the transcendental, non-material definition of the individual.[35]

What is Unique About the Human Species as Distinct From Nonhuman Living Organisms?

After considering all of the above, a response to this question is clearly as complex as it is controversial. The non-believing materialist will adopt a position that the human being is simply a highly evolved animal at the apex of the evolutionary tree, whose intelligence and consciousness is merely a product of a highly developed brain, explicable through purely biological and evolutionary mechanisms. The believing theist will contend that humans are a special creation of the Creator, as per scriptural revelation, having a unique mind found in no other animal and a supernatural soul which is non-material. Even in the biological evolutionary space, humans are like no other species in a number of other respects. Firstly, it is a moot point whether humans are still evolving. It could be argued that the engine that drives evolution—selective pressure to propagate advantageous traits—is not operative in the human world of advanced medical science, social outreach, and a population growth which is inversely proportional to affluence and advantage. Studies of human populations to detect evolution-driven genetic variations would be difficult to carry out and would

---

32. b. Berachot 57b.
33. Scherman, *Complete Artscroll Siddur*, 18.
34. HaLevi, *Kuzari*, 521–22.

35. On a more amusing note—Dr. Duncan MacDougall experimented with 6 terminally ill patients in April 1901 to try and determine the weight of the human soul by weighing these individuals before and after death when the soul left the body. He concluded that the human soul weighed on average 21grams. See "Soul Has Weight."

require very large population samples. A recent study did look at the DNA of 215,000 people, searching for genetic markers that could affect longevity.[36] They found several of these markers accumulating in samples of the elderly. These were interpreted to indicate an increasing enrichment of the human gene pool for favorable traits on the basis of the grandmother hypothesis, i.e., healthy parents and grandparents would increase the chances of survival and further reproduction of the younger generation. What is not controversial is the profound impact of humans on the ecosystem of the planet, as referred to above with respect to the epoch of the Anthropocene. The fallout from human domination of the planet, as alluded to in Gen 1:28, has taken on immense proportions. The majority of large animals in the wild have been replaced by artificially-bred domesticated animal life, and the major portion of the pristine forests and savanna have been overrun by agricultural development. Science has provided the human species with a special force to drastically change the planet. Inarguably, in this respect, the human species stands alone.

---

36. Mostafavi et al., "Identifying Genetic Variants," 1–29.

5

Non-Predicate Theism

> But He said: 'you cannot see My face, for man may not see Me and live
>
> —Exod 33:20

Non-predicate Theism—Introduction

WE HAVE SEEN IN chapters 2 to 4 how the science narrative has spawned a body of searching questions that demand to be addressed. The following two chapters will seek to explore responses from a theistic standpoint. How is God perceived by humankind, and how does God, as understood by religious revelation, communicate to humankind?

The premise on which I have proposed the concept of non-predicate theism relates to the incapacity of humankind to assign attributes to God. Ludwig Wittgenstein has contended that human language is founded on pictorial imagery, developed from our sensory experiences.[1] However, the realm of the Divine lies in a wholly different domain, beyond human language, cognition, and understanding and, therefore, any attributes we assign to God are invalid. Nevertheless, it is an axiom of religious belief that God has, and does, communicate to humans—the components of divine revelation will be discussed in chapter 6. Revelation and communication, of course, need to be in the medium understood by humans—i.e., in anthropomorphic terms. Non-predicate theism

---

1. Wittgenstein, *Tractatus Logico-Philosophicus*, 2.063–2.225.

is the proposition that anthropomorphic terminology should not be conflated with divine attributes. Thus, while God's creation of the world and God's communication and revelation are predicates of God's relationship to humankind, the ideology of belief in God, i.e., theism, is not qualified with a human comprehensible predicate—hence non-predicate theism.

It is generally accepted in the three Abrahamic monotheistic religions, that humans have no sensate conception of God. The personality, characteristics, behavior, and activities of God are portrayed in human language for human cognition and understanding. On occasion, the deficiencies of human language give rise to apparent contradictions and misunderstandings, often providing fuel for non-believers to attack religion. Wittgenstein's theory of language would not find this too surprising. In the *Tractatus*, Wittgenstein's monumental philosophical work, his pictorial theory of language proposes that facts are pictures—they might not look like pictures, but once they are analyzed or decomposed they form a set of elementary statements that are pictures.[2] Thus, any utterance about the world can be dissected into words that are names of things, and thereby the relationship is formed between the words in the sentence.

> The sum-total of reality is the world. We picture facts to ourselves. A picture presents a situation in logical space, the existence and non-existence of states of affairs. A picture is a model of reality. In a picture objects have the elements of the picture corresponding to them. In a picture the elements of the picture are the representatives of objects. What constitutes a picture is that its elements are related to one another in a determinate way. A picture is a fact. The fact that the elements of a picture are related to one another in a determinate way represents that things are related to one another in the same way. Let us call this connexion of its elements the structure of the picture, and let us call the possibility of this structure the pictorial form of the picture. Pictorial form is the possibility that things are related to one another in the same

2. Wittgenstein, *Tractatus Logico-Philosophicus*, 2.063–2.225.

way as the elements of the picture. That is how a picture is attached to reality; it reaches right out to it.[3]

The monotheistic God of the Judaic-Christian-Muslim faiths is an invisible Deity—invisible to human cognition, who cannot be pictured in any sense. Human language is therefore deficient in describing attributions of God. However, in order to establish a relationship with God, various anthropomorphic attributions have been utilized in religious teachings and literature. These attributions couched in human language are not attributes of God—humans do not have the ability to "know" God's attributes. For this reason I prefer the term "attribution" rather than "attributes" to assign human descriptions of the activities and communications from God to humans. This leads to the definition of the term "non-predicate theism"—as discussed above in the introduction. It is imperative that I re-emphasize that "non-predicate" qualifies the ideology of theism, but not any feature to be attributed to the personal God, where clearly "non-predicate" is not appropriate.

The rational pathway to belief would generally commence with pondering the existential questions, followed by the questions of religious belief, and then leading onto the revealed religions.

Why Existence?

Since the dawn of humankind, *Homo sapiens* has pondered, reflected, and wondered about the ontological question of his/her environment—not only the tangible measurable sensate environment, but what might lie beyond that physical environment. Questions such as these still remain in the philosophical minds of today's scientific and technologically sophisticated human community. Why is there existence? Why is there something rather than nothing? What lies beyond human cognition, conception, comprehension, and speculation? Can today's science have an approach to answer these questions?

---

3. Wittgenstein, *Tractatus Logico-Philosophicus*, 2.063–2.1511.

Contemporary existential epistemology is divided into firstly, the physicalists or materialists, who hold that everything supervenes on the physical,[4] and that science is the sole purveyor of truth. This viewpoint, as detailed in the introductory chapter, is one which is widely accepted in the scientific community. Alternately, there is the standpoint of dualism, in which reality consists of both a natural component, amenable to scientific investigation and scientific knowledge, as well as an extra-natural or supernatural component of reality, which is beyond the reach of human scientific investigation.

Why Religion?

Religion, in its various guises throughout the history of humankind, arose to address the human quest to try and understand the mysteries of the universe. Religion has also provided the vehicle to comfort and give security from the unknown terrors of the night, and was, and still is, also a powerful tool to promote social coherence. The three monotheistic religions, Judaism, Christianity, and Islam, each claim their authenticity from direct communication from God through their specific revelations. (Divine revelation will be dealt with more fully in chapter 6.) What has developed in all three religions are conceptions of God packaged into human language in order to be comprehended through human understanding. These anthropomorphic analogies and attributions, because of the deficiencies of human language, have provided to the non-believer a major resource for criticism and attack of religious faith.

Human Conceptions of God

In most (but not all) religious systems, it is believed that no human after biblical/qur'anic times has had direct communication from God. In the Jewish tradition, God's revelation to humans has been direct via the revelation at Mount Sinai, as well as through the

---

4. Stoljar, "Physicalism."

prophets, and also from the Torah, which occupies a pivotal role in the Jewish religion. Outside of the revelations of the recognized religious faiths, human claims to have had direct communication with God are treated with skepticism and kindly recommendations to seek professional help. Human recognition of the supernatural God cannot, by definition, be empirical. The five so-called "attributes" of God, prefixed by omni-, are human linguistic descriptions of God's actions and particularities:

1. Omnipotence—that God is all-powerful
2. Omniscient—that God is all-knowing
3. Omni-benevolent—that God is all kind and all good
4. Omni-temporal—that God exists in all times
5. Omni-present—that God exists in all places

Numerous scriptural references allude to these attributions, and have been universally accepted in all monotheistic faiths to characterize God's relationship to his earthly creatures. While these five are commonly described as "attributes" it needs to be re-emphasized that they are anthropomorphic analogues to facilitate human comprehension. A better and more precise terminology would be that they are "anthropomorphic attributions." The exercise of assigning human analogical attributions to God, which feature strongly in prayer, are vehicles to assist human supplication to God.

Divine Impenetrability

How does one define the relationship that needs to be established between natural humans and the supernatural Creator, as it is a positive commandment to "know" God? However, the hiddenness of God, the *Deus Absconditus*, immediately poses a significant challenge when trying to define God in human terminology. Of course, much has come down through revelation and the holy Scriptures of the various religions, in particular through the studies of sages and through their interpretation within their respective theological spheres. I have mentioned above in chapter 1 the difficulties of the human mind to satisfactorily define the concepts of "infinity," "always," "limitless space and time," etc. Similarly, in regard to the noetic essence of God, this has been concealed and is not comprehensible to the human mind. Some of these examples, when translated to a human conceptual level, are incomprehensible. How can there be a divine oversight of the universality of humankind, necessary to comply with each individual's religious accountability? How does the universal divine presence comply with unitary indivisibility—a cardinal requirement of monotheism? How does one comprehend what is stated in the daily service of the Jewish prayer book, that God re-creates the world every day?[5] What is the meaning of the concept that God created the world by his spoken word, as mentioned in Gen 1 "and God said ..." for each of his creations?

Divine Simplicity

The concept of divine simplicity, which at first blush may appear to be a rather incongruous combination, or even oxymoronic, has been an essential component of classical theism. For a review of the idea of divine simplicity see Brian Davies's *An Introduction to the Philosophy of Religion*, chapter 8.[6] God's perfection implies his immutability and his externality from his created world where changes occur. These constituents of divine simplicity do raise a number of philosophical challenges. For example, does immutability compromise God's ability to create? God's immutability is confirmed in the Scriptures by the prophet Malachi (Mal 3:6): "for I am the Lord—I have not changed." And yet the Bible documents several instances where God would appear to change his plans. For example, in Exod 32:10, following on the sin of the golden calf by the Israelites soon after receiving the tablets of the Ten

---

5. Scherman, *Complete Artscroll Siddur*, 84, 88.
6. Davies, *Introduction*, 158–80.

Commandments, God declares to his prophet Moses, "Now let Me be, that My anger may blaze forth against them and that I may destroy them, and make of you a great nation." Moses then intervenes on behalf of his people and pleads for God's mercy, and four verses later, in Exod 32:14: "And the Lord renounced the punishment He had planned to bring upon His people."

Divine simplicity also implies his absolute indivisibility. "Hear O Israel the Lord our God the Lord is one" is the single most important verse in the entire Jewish liturgy. It is biblically commanded for a Jew to say it three times a day, and it is also said before retiring at night. It is the last words on the lips of a Jewish soul when departing this earthly existence, and it was on the lips of thousands of martyrs before being murdered. Not the slightest deviation from the unitary, indivisible attribute of God is tolerated—it is one of the three cardinal sins for which a Jew is obliged to give up his life rather than to surrender to. Indivisibility implies that there is no distinction between God and his "attributes"; His nature, essence, and existence are all the same. Clearly the linkage of the concept of indivisibility with that of cosmic universality lies beyond human comprehension.

The Omni- Attributes

The five omni- attributes mentioned above have traditionally been part of the creed of all three monotheistic religions. Numerous allusions to all five of these attributes occur in the holy Scriptures and in prayer services. The omni- attributes, however, being human linguistic creations, cause difficulties with logical interpretations of meaning. Ludwig Wittgenstein has quipped with regard to philosophy: "philosophy is a battle against the bewitchment of our intelligence by means of language."[7] It applies no less to the philosophy of religion. So, for example, it would appear that divine omniscience suggests a deterministic compromise of freewill, which ought to be a cardinal requirement for religious

---

7. Wittgenstein, *Philosophical Investigations*, 109, 47.

accountability. Put another way, does it imply that human actions are determined by God's foreknowledge? (This criticism can be rebutted by the understanding that knowledge and causation are not the same. In other words—my actions are not contingent on God's knowledge of the future, as he is not bound by time and would have knowledge of future happenings without necessarily modifying them.) From Maimonides, " . . . according to the teaching of our Law, God's knowledge of one of two eventualities does not determine it, however certain that knowledge may be concerning the future occurrence of the one eventuality."[8] Similarly, does God's omniscience mean that supplicatory prayers are meaningless, as the future is already set by God's will, irrespective of our petition? (Rebutted by the supposition that God's will for the future could be determined by His evaluation of the supplication for a future outcome.) An old chestnut to challenge God's omnipotence is whether He can create something He cannot destroy, or more commonly put—can God create a stone He cannot lift? (Rebutted as it is a fallacy of logic—by positioning two contrasting questions as one question.)

Numerous other contrivances of language aimed at attacking religion utilize either logical fallacies or are directed at divine "attributes" often employing the trick of deceptively combining these "attributes" together. To illustrate, it may be worth mentioning the Euthyphro dilemma[9]—originally formulated by Socrates. In a more modern form it poses the question—is X good because God has endowed it with goodness, or is X intrinsically good and, therefore, God endorses its goodness? The former questions the omni-benevolence attribute of God employing selected scriptural passages to display brutality and cruelty (for example, the wholesale slaughter of the Midianites in Num 31:17 and the

---

8. Maimonides, *Guide for the Perplexed* 3:20, 294.

9. The Euthyphro dilemma is a story related by Plato regarding a meeting between Socrates and Euthyphro. Socrates is being charged with impiety and Euthyphro has come to prosecute his father on the dubious charge of the unintentional murder of a thug. Socrates inquires of Euthyphro if the pious are loved by the gods because it is pious or is it pious because it is loved by the gods. *Plato, Euthyphro.*

Amalekites in 1 Sam 15:3). The latter query of the Euthyphro dilemma would imply that goodness lies external to God thus weakening all three of his attributes of omnipotence, omniscience, and omni-benevolence.

All of the above examples are essentially in the Wittgensteinian mold of language manipulation and are interesting, if not entertaining, exercises in attack and rebuttal. A far more fundamental challenge to theism is the problem of evil and theodicy.

The Challenge of Evil

The word "evil" connotes pointless suffering that is, at least, significant in extent. It is commonly divided into moral evil, perpetrated on humans and animals by humans, and natural evils, resulting from natural occurrences and disasters. Many examples of both evils come easily to mind. That God alone is ultimately responsible for everything in the world, both good and evil,[10] is reflected in a special blessing in the Jewish tradition which is made on hearing bad tidings, "Blessed are you O Lord our God, King of the universe, the true judge," the formula of submission to God's will. In the Scriptures, the paradigmatic book of Job describes the succession of one affliction after the other suffered by the character Job, whose faith is tested by God.

The major challenge to religious belief is the clearly visible presence of pointless suffering in the world. As expressed over two thousand years ago by the ancient Greek philosopher, Epicurus (341–270 BCE):

> Is God willing to prevent evil, but not able? Then he is not omnipotent.
> Is he able, but not willing? Then he is malevolent.
> Is he both able and willing? Then whence cometh evil?
> Is he neither able nor willing? Then why call him God?[11]

---

10. The Maharal, *Tiferet Yisrael*, 230.
11. Wikiquote, "Epicurus."

In more recent times, the most direct logic justifying atheism based on the challenge of evil, is articulated in the inductive argument of William L. Rowe (1931-2015).[12] The first premise is that there are many examples of pointless suffering in the world. The second premise is that if there is a God who is purported to be omniscient, he would know all about suffering. If he was omnipotent, he would be able to prevent or stop it or, at the least, greatly ameliorate the suffering. If he was omni-benevolent, he would strive to stop the suffering. The conclusion, therefore, is that, because there is a great deal of pointless suffering in the world, there is no omni-God.

The theistic defense against the challenges of evil is termed "theodicy"—defined as the theological defense of God's attributes in view of the existence of evil. The subject is large and complex and what follows is a brief summary in order to relate the challenge to the proposition of non-predicate theism.

> The believer in God must account for the existence of unjust suffering; the atheist has to account for everything else.[13]
>
> —Milton Steinberg (1903-1950).

The three foremost defenses in the literature of theodicy come from John H. Hick (1922-2012), Alvin C. Plantinga (1932-), and Gottfried Wilhelm Leibniz (1646-1716):

The Soul-Making Theodicy of Hick[14]

Hick uses the analogy of good parents who would not want their child to be free of any challenges or pain during the child's life, as adversity and, consequently, moral responsibility promote virtue and build a better person. It is those trials and tribulations throughout life, which must include setbacks and some suffering that build character and moral virtue. In addition, evil also

---

12. Bergmann, "Skeptical Theism," 278-96.
13. Steinberg, "Believer in God."
14. Hick, *Philosophy of Religion*, 117.

provides opportunities for the development and exhibition of humanity, charity, and benevolence. A criticism of Hicks's theodicy raises the question of how God obtained his own moral virtue. Clearly God would have supreme moral virtue, but on the other hand not through suffering. Why couldn't the same apply for humans and free humans from suffering? More fundamentally, if God is the supreme moral virtue, where was his intervention in the most anguished sufferings, for example the Holocaust? A parent standing by a child's suffering to this degree could hardly be called a good loving parent or acting in the child's best interests.

The Freewill Theodicy of Plantinga[15]

The most commonly cited defense of theodicy is the requirement for freewill. The requirement for freewill, which encompasses virtue and evil, good and bad, pleasure and suffering, is an essential component of religious responsibility and accountability, and, therefore, reward and punishment. The need for freewill outweighs the consequences of suffering. However, this theodicy defense is incomplete as it addresses only moral evil and not natural evil.

This is the Best of All Possible Worlds Theodicy of Leibniz[16]

Leibniz's theodicy defense presupposes the existence of God, and posits that God has freely chosen this world from all possibilities. Mere mortals are not able to see the big picture, and irrespective of what happens, everything is for the greater good, even if it is not apparent immediately. This is analogous to a beautiful tapestry, which, on the reverse side, is merely a messy jumble of loose threads. The difficulty with Leibniz's defense is that, like a

---

15. Plantinga, *Free-Will Defence*, 167–86.
16. See Leibniz, "Theodicy," 218–36.

conspiracy theory, it is founded on speculation, which is non-evidential and non-disconfirmable.[17]

Debates and arguments continue between theists and atheists on the challenge of evil to religious belief. Theists rationalize that pain and suffering is often a prelude to a greater good. For example, one could cite medical examples ranging from the sting of a vaccine injection to the suffering of chemotherapy, which are ultimately for the outcome of good. A more profound theodicy defense is the assurance of ultimate reward in the world to come. This is also the common defense for the troubling, frequently occurring, conundrum of the apparent suffering of the righteous and the apparent reward of the wicked. The arguments of the non-believer that are based on evil remain significant challenges to the theist, and, especially, defending natural evil, more so than moral evil, as well as the extent of suffering that is necessary for a greater good.

Negative Theology

It is clear that descriptions of God by human language are incompetent, which has led to the articulation of negative theology.[18] Negative theology, also known as apophatic theology or theology by negation, has been a concept in theology since earliest times. The early Christian theologian, Pseudo-Dionysius the Areopagite, in the late fifth to early sixth century, wrote that God is beyond the reach of human language—beyond both affirmation and negation. In the Middle Ages, St. Thomas Aquinas emphasized that in contrast to creatures, God is not composed of anything, and therefore no form of language is able to describe him. All forms of speech distinguish components of things, and God is not composed of parts.

Maimonides was the major proponent of negative theology in the Jewish religion. He rejects emphatically the assigning of attributes to God:

---

17. To disconfirm means to show that a hypothesis or a belief is not true or may not be true (Oxford Dictionary).
18. Milem, "Four Theories," 187–204.

If, however, you have a desire to rise to a higher state, viz., that of reflection, and truly to hold the conviction that God is One and possesses true unity, without admitting plurality or divisibility in any sense whatever, you must understand that God has no essential attribute in any form or in any sense whatever, and that the rejection of corporeality implies the rejection of essential attributes.[19]

God's transcendence precludes our ability to speak of his attributes using language of this world. In Maimonidean negative theology, we are not competent to describe God in terms of all-powerful and all-knowing with regard to being at the apex of substances, as even "substance" cannot be predicated of God.[20] With regard to applying predicates to God, Maimonides wrote:

> ... the cause of the error of all these schools is their belief that God's knowledge is like ours; each school points to something withheld from our knowledge and either assumes that the same must be the case in God's knowledge, or at least finds some difficulty how to explain it... How then can they imagine that they comprehend His knowledge which is identical with His essence; seeing that our incapacity to comprehend His essence prevents us from understanding the way how He knows objects? for His knowledge is not the same kind as ours but totally different from it and admitting of no analogy ... The homonymity of the term "knowledge" misled people; [they forgot that] only the words are the same but the things designated by them are different; and therefore they came to the absurd conclusion that that which is required for our knowledge is also required for God's knowledge...[21]

---

19. Maimonides, *Guide for the Perplexed* 1:50, 67.
20. Seeskin, "Maimonides."
21. Maimonides, *Guide for the Perplexed* 3:20, 293.

Non-Predicate Theism

The concept of non-predicate theism derives from the negative theology of Maimonides and similar ideas expressed by a number of other philosophers and theologians. Creaturely language cannot comprehend the creator—this has led to the numerous examples of anthropomorphic fallacy. However, communication from God to humans through the medium of the Scriptures, has, of necessity, come through anthropomorphic language, suited to convey in human terms his activities and spiritual truths. However, it is an error to predicate attributes of God, or to interpret these anthropomorphic attributions of God, as his attributes. The term "non-predicate theism" is aimed at more precisely portraying this reality, rather than the term "negative theology" which could be misunderstood as a denial of a divine relationship with humanity.

Non-predicate theism responds to the challenges created by the assigning of "attributes" to God, as discussed above. However, what of the serious challenge of evil? This is clearly not an easy challenge to dismiss even though many rebuttals have been attempted, such as the few mentioned above. Non-predicate theism implies that humans are incompetent to comprehend God's intentions, which would include those occurrences and events which appear to humans as pointless suffering. It is true that the challenge of defending the serious problem of seemingly pointless evil is often avoided by sheltering under the apology of "God's workings are unknown" or "we are unable to fathom the why's of God's reasons." Worryingly for theism, it may appear to be the easy way out for the inability to rationally respond to the challenge. This is not too dissimilar to the similarly shallow response of Job to God's test of faith. However, negative theology has responded to the challenge of opting out of a response by countering that the incomprehensibility of the Lord, and what goes with this position, is, in fact, knowledge itself.[22] Nevertheless incomprehensibility and inability of understanding the Divine

---

22. Adams, "Predication," 235–83.

does leave open the difficulty of burden of proof for something which humans have no coherent explanation.

Non-Predicate Theism—Conclusion

For the religious believer, God clearly has absolute and total ownership, authority and control of the natural world he created. However, the linguistic construct of labeling this attribute as "omnipotent" is an anthropomorphic fallacy, which can lead to simplistic physical imagery (such as the creation-lifting stone "paradox" mentioned above). Similarly, as God created all that constitutes the natural world, including the creation of time, God is knowledgeable of every occurrence in every individual component of the world—a concept beyond human comprehension. Labeling this attribute as "omniscient" is similarly an anthropomorphic fallacy. The linguistic qualification of "omni-benevolent" is also an attribute that lies beyond human conception, as is God's purpose and plan for the universe God created. Arguments around theodicy, as discussed above, may well be learned academic pursuits, but remain anthropomorphic speculation. For this reason, the ideology of theism needs the qualification of excluding anthropomorphic predication.

6

Divine Revelation

> Because the truth is certain that the Holy One blessed is He could have created His world in an all-encompassing way . . . it would not be possible for us to understand His way at all, . . . His capability cannot be grasped by our intellect, and cannot be understood by man whose knowledge is limited by its specific rules. But because the Heavenly will wanted man to be able to understand a small part of His ways and actions . . . therefore He gave us room to contemplate them, and to understand at least a tiny part, if not the enormous [whole].[1]
>
> —R' Moshe Chaim Luzzatto (1707–1746)

Divine—Human Communication

We have seen in the previous chapter aspects of the human perceptions of God. What of the reverse—the communication from God to humankind through revelation in its various religious configurations? Revelation via human language constitutes the centrality of the three monotheistic religions. However the canon of revelations, of course, does vary widely between the different formal monotheistic religions. What is common to all theistic belief systems is that revelation plays the pivotal role in religious conviction. Revelation, God's communication to humans, is the

---

1. Luzzatto, *Da'at Tevunot*, [53](40).

common article of faith which completes the validation of the truth of divine existence. It is beyond the scope of this book to analyze why there are such different perceptions of divine revelation, expressed through fairly widely differing religious structures and followings. However, the fact that there are so many widely differing and competing doctrines which are, in a number of cases, even mutually exclusive, is a weakness of theism and often recognized as such by atheism. As I come from the Orthodox Jewish background, I will give a brief account of our appraisal of God's revelation to humans through the Jewish religion.

Prophetic Revelation

Prophetic revelation can be considered on three levels—firstly, the revelation at Mount Sinai, when God directly communicated to the Children of Israel, the entire nation reaching the level of prophecy; secondly, the special prophecy of Moses; and thirdly, divine communication to the other prophets.

The revelation at Sinai was a unique event in human history, when the voice of God was heard by an entire nation of millions of people, amid an awe-inspiring background of lightning, thunder, the mountain on fire and smoking, and loud continual blaring from the ram's horn. The entire nation heard God communicating the first two of the Ten Commandments (in Judaism it is more correctly translated as the "Ten Statements," as there are in fact 613 commandments, the ten merely forming the fundamental set carved into the tablets). With the first two commandments there was no intermediary between God and human, and the entire population heard God's "voice." The awesomeness compelled the frightened people to request Moses to be the intermediary for the remaining eight Commandments.

Following the national revelation at Sinai, God would communicate to the Children of Israel through prophets. These were selected men and women, well over a million of them, some of whose writings form part of the Bible. However, the prophecy of Moses was unlike that of the other prophets as elaborated in the holy Scriptures and in the seventh principle of the thirteen Principles of Faith of Maimonides.[2] The unique prophecy of Moses is unequivocally spelt out in the Bible in several instances. In Num 12:6–8, God declares: "When a prophet of the Lord arises among you, I make Myself known to him in a vision, I speak with him in a dream. Not so with My servant Moses... With him I speak mouth to mouth, plainly and not in riddles, and he beholds the likeness of the Lord." The written Torah (the so-called five books of Moses) concludes in Deut 34:10, "Never again did there arise in Israel a prophet like Moses—whom the Lord singled out face to face."

Men and women chosen to be prophets had, step-by-step over time, attained the supreme level of moral perfection.[3] These prophets would receive their Divine message while in a trance-like state or in a dream, and also when summoned by God. The message would be cryptic, requiring the prophet to interpret it. Moses, however, would receive verbal communication directly from God, while fully conscious and alert. He was also able to communicate with God at will. According to Jewish tradition, prophecy ceased about 2,500 years ago with the death of the last prophet, Malachi.

Revelation Through the Torah

The Torah is a crucial component of Jewish religion. "God granted us one particular means which can bring man close to God more than anything else. This is the study of His revealed Torah."[4] The Torah consists of two elements of equal status, equal sanctity, and equal importance—the Written Torah and the Oral Torah. The Written Torah, comprised of the five books of Moses, is believed to be the direct word of God, dictated by God to Moses and subsequently written down by Moses. Each word of the Written Torah carries with it the sanctity of being a direct communication from God, and is therefore read with exact precision in the Torah

2. Kaplan, *Maimonides' Principles*, 53–59.
3. Luzzatto, *Way of God*, 215.
4. Luzzatto, *Way of God*, 71.

DIVINE REVELATION

readings that form part of the synagogue service. Simultaneously Moses received directly from God, the Oral Torah—the major source of Jewish law and a vital part of Jewish theology. It is called the Oral Torah as it was never meant to be committed to writing but would be taught verbally from rabbinic authorities and sages to their students through the generations. However, following the destruction of the Second Temple, in the year 70 CE, and the persecutions and travails that beset the Jewish communities, there was a fear that the Oral Torah could be lost. Consequently, one of the towering personalities of Jewish history following the destruction of the Second Temple, Yehuda HaNasi ("Judah the Prince"), undertook the task of committing the Oral Torah to writing, and thus was born the Mishnah, in approximately 190 CE. Consisting of terse succinct summaries of Jewish legal jurisprudence, the integrity of the Oral Torah still remained largely dependent on generational transmission. The scholars of the Mishnaic period were known as Tannaim ("teachers"). This period stretched from 10 to 200 CE.[5] In the ensuing years, it soon became apparent that survival of the Oral Torah could also be vulnerable to the upheavals and disruptions, which, sadly, became the lot of the Jewish people. The Tannaim were succeeded by the Amoraim ("explainers" or "interpreters") from 200 to 475 CE. It was the Amoraim who then took the discussions and explanations of the Mishnaic texts and recorded them in what became known as the Gemara. The Talmud is the combination of the Mishnah and the Gemara. There are two versions of the Talmud, one originating from Babylon, the Babylonian Talmud, and one from Israel, the Jerusalem Talmud. The Talmud was then sealed and no further additions were permitted. In the ensuing centuries right down to the present time, numerous scholarly works by sages have commented, discussed, analyzed, dissected, and elaborated on the Talmud, to produce the vast Jewish religious scholarly literature extant today, and studied in thousands of Yeshivas and other institutes of learning throughout the world. In addition, the laws have been codified from the

---

5. Spiro, *Crash Course*, 204.

Talmud for easier reference by scholars recognized as the authorities of their respective eras.

So elevated is the Torah in the Jewish tradition that it is believed that the Torah predated the creation of the universe,[6] and that God looked to the Torah as the blueprint for the creation.[7] Ludwig Wittgenstein has stated skeptically "how things are in the world is a matter of complete indifference for what is higher. God is not to reveal himself in the world."[8] In contrast to this, the Jewish position is unequivocal that God has communicated of himself and continues to do so through the Torah—for "the Torah speaks the language of man."[9]

The Written Torah, or "Old Testament" of the Bible, is more familiar than the Oral Torah to those outside of the Jewish religion and comprises narrative, allegory, moral injunctions, and laws. However, much of the legal component of the Jewish religion, i.e., the ordinances God requires of observant Jews, is not derived directly from the often obscure hints in the Written Torah. As an example, the requirements for the kosher slaughter of animals in Deut 12:21 states " . . . you may slaughter any of the cattle or sheep that the Lord gives you, as I have instructed you." However, the details of these instructions are not provided anywhere in the Written Torah. The explicit details were conveyed verbally by God to Moses in the Oral Torah. Simple interpretations of the Written Torah are often incorrect or misleading as to the message which God has conveyed. For example, the injunction in Exod 21:24 of an "eye for an eye" is explicated in the Oral Torah as a legal statement, and must not be taken literally. It is incorrect to interpret this to mean that the eye of the perpetrator should be damaged to an equivalent degree as to what was done to the victim. What is explained by the Oral Torah is that the injunction refers to the total monetary value of the injury, i.e., the costs of treatment,

---

6. Chofetz Chaim, *Blueprint for Creation*.
7. Appelson, *Greenway*.
8. Wittgenstein, *Tractatus Logico-Philosophicus* 6.432, 88.
9. b. Berachot 33b.

rehabilitation, loss of income, etc., which has to be paid by the perpetrator to the victim.

Many laws given by God have obvious rational reasons for societal well-being and for harmonious human-to-human relations. However, for many other laws the underlying reasons have not been revealed to mortals. They are observed from conviction that they emanate from God's communication to humanity, and are instructions from God that are beyond the ambit of human understanding.

The Talmud consists of discussions, debates, allegories, and other instruments to establish the legal and ethical messages communicated by God to humans. The study of Torah is thus a crucial requirement for the observant Jew. To illustrate this—a part of the regular daily morning service includes an extract from the Gemara which gives a list of examples of positive commandments, such as honoring parents, hospitality, visiting the sick, attention and devotion while praying, and others. Importantly, this passage from the Gemara concludes with a statement that the study of Torah is equivalent to them all.[10]

Revelation Through Miracles

Revelation through miracles resonates prominently through all monotheistic faiths. Indeed, all three monotheistic religions were founded on miracles—for example, the resurrection of Jesus, Muhammed receiving the Qur'an from the angel Jibreel, and the revelation at Sinai, respectively for Christianity, Islam, and Judaism. Miracles are generally, but importantly not always, taken to be a proof of a religious message from God by followers of all three religions. (An important exception mentioned in the Bible in Deut 13:2, 3 warns against the false prophet, who may well demonstrate miracles to support his attempt to seduce people to believe in idolatry. He should not be followed, and he should be put to death.)

---

10. b. Shabbat 127a.

How is a miracle defined? In common usage a miracle is an unusual, fortuitous, and usually favorable event. David Hume's definition is well-known: "a miracle is a violation of the laws of nature . . . Nothing is esteemed a miracle, if it ever happens in the common course of nature."[11] The religious definition of a miracle also incorporates the violation of natural laws and the defiance of any scientific explanation, but also specifies that it is brought about by God in order to convey a religious message. Religious miracles can be divided, firstly into private miracles—revealed to one or a few individuals, and then propagated to many by testimony; and secondly, public miracles—revealed directly, and simultaneously, to a very large number of people, or a nation. Both forms of miracles have protagonists and skeptics or detractors.

Private Miracles

Private miracles may be perceived in various ways:

1. **The fortuitous miracle.** An example of this is the well-known humorous Texan sharpshooter fallacy, where a Texan, observing a cluster of bullet holes in a barn wall, draws a circle around them and announces that he is a sharpshooter.[12] This fallacy is an example of artificially, after the fact, making a fortuitous event into an improbability or a "miracle."

2. **The fraudulent miracle.** Many a fake pastor throughout the world has relieved gullible audiences of their money by trickery and deception, often with plants in the audience, claiming to communicate with God and perform "miracles," poignantly including "miracle healings."

3. **The mistaken miracle.** The perceptual bias to over-detect agents in the environment as religious miracles has been postulated to be a consequence of the evolution of religion.[13]

---

11. Hume, "Enquiry Concerning Human Understanding," 79.
12. Wikipedia, "Texas Sharpshooter Fallacy."
13. Van Elk et al., "Priming of Supernatural Agent Detection," 4–33.

The perception of "miraculous" religious imagery in natural phenomena is known as religious pareidolia. Many believers view them as real manifestations of miraculous origin. Two of the many examples are: the grilled cheese image of the Virgin Mary, which was sold on eBay for $28,000;[14] the image formed by salt deposits on an overpass in Chicago, which became known as Our Lady of the Overpass, and for a time was a site of local Catholic pilgrimage.[15]

4. **The embedded miracle.** These are miracles that form a constituent part of religious belief. One of the most famous Catholic pilgrimage sites in the world is Lourdes—a town in southwestern France. It was here, in 1858, where an uneducated 14-year-old girl from an impoverished family claimed to have witnessed eighteen visions of the Virgin Mary. The grotto is visited by nearly 6 million people annually, many seeking miraculous cures. A forty-member medical team found that, since 1858, of the thousands of alleged medical "cures," only 69 could be medically authenticated and none since 1976 (up to the time of the study in 2006).[16]

The fragility of the private miracle rests on the reliability of testimony. David Hume cautioned that testimony should only be trusted if one has evidence that the testifier is likely to be right or, if what is being testified, is likely to be right.

> Suppose, for instance, that the fact, which the testimony endeavors to establish, partakes of the extraordinary and the marvelous; in that case the evidence resulting from the testimony admits of a diminution, greater or less, in proportion as the fact is more or less unusual.[17]

In other words, the more unusual or unnatural the claim that is made, the less likely it is to be believed. In either event, belief in

---

14. BBC, "Virgin Mary" Toast.
15. Wikipedia, "Our Lady of the Underpass."
16. Francois et al., "Lourdes Medical Cures," 135–62.
17. Hume, "Enquiry Concerning Human Understanding," 78.

a private miracle depends on the credibility of the testimony and trustworthiness of the witness.

Public Miracles

Public miracles, unlike private miracles, are at an advantage for reliability in not having to depend on testimony. However, there have been no public miracles, i.e., miracles witnessed and experienced by an entire population or nation, since biblical times. The authenticity of public miracles rests on national memory of the miracle. Perhaps the most well-known argument for the credibility of public miracles, specifically the miracles experienced by the Children of Israel as detailed in the Bible, is what has come to be known as the Kuzari principle. *The Kuzari,* written by the poet, philosopher, physician Rabbi Yehuda HaLevi (c. 1075–1141) is one of the most well-known and well-loved philosophical works of Judaism.[18] The book is an allegorical dialogue between a seventh-century central Asian king and representatives of different faiths—but predominantly the Jewish faith. The king and his entire nation is then purported to have converted to Judaism. The fundamental idea put forward in the *Kuzari* is that a miracle of enormous proportions and great relevance, which is experienced by an entire nation and is recorded and passed on from generation to generation, cannot be a fabricated myth. It is interesting to compare this attribute of a public miracle with that of a private miracle, as incorporated by Hume into his definition of a miracle. As mentioned above, Hume stated that the more unusual an event, the less likely it is believed to be a miracle.[19] With a public miracle, the more unusual an event the less likely it is to be a fabricated myth, and the more likely it is to be historically authentic. Several public miracles witnessed and experienced by the entire nation of Israel are discussed in the *Kuzari,* such as the revelation at Sinai,

---

18. HaLevi, *Kuzari* 1:84, 97.
19. Hume, "Enquiry Concerning Human Understanding," 78.

the provision of the manna in the desert to sustain the entire nation, and the parting of the Red Sea.[20]

> This detailed narration of chronicles in your Torah removes any suspicion of falsification or mass conspiracy. ... Eventually the lie would be exposed. At the very least, anyone who would try to substantiate the lie would be disproved. And if this applies to just 10 people... Imagine how impossible it would be to proliferate a lie of this kind among an entire generation of people.[21]

The modern version of the Kuzari principle has been developed by Rabbi Dovid Gottlieb (1950-) and similarly aims to support the authenticity of the public miracles of the Bible.[22] The Kuzari argument in its updated version posits that a miracle witnessed and experienced by a very large number of people, in this case the entire nation of the Children of Israel of some 3 million souls, will be retained in the national memory to the present time, provided certain definitional criteria are met. These are, firstly, the need for a very large mass of individuals simultaneously witnessing the purported miracle. Secondly, the miracle is of a very impressionable and very unusual nature. Thirdly, the miracle is recorded immediately by the generation experiencing the miracle and is then passed on faithfully to succeeding generations. Fourthly, members of the current generation having the memory of the miracle are the direct descendants of the original generation who experienced the miracle. There have been a number of attempts to rebut the argument,[23] but in the main, the rebuttals have not complied totally with the required criteria of the argument.[24] Some of the rebuttals refer to myth and legend formation seen in many other cultures from that period of time. However, myth formation would imply that the purported miracle was introduced by the author of the myth into a society who

20. HaLevi, *Kuzari* 1:84, 97.
21. HaLevi, *Kuzari* 1:48, 76
22. Gottlieb, *Living up to the Truth*, 32.
23. Tanner, "Refuting the Kuzari Principle."
24. Gottlieb, "Living up to the Truth."

subsequently accepted it, i.e., a societal-accepted private miracle, rather than a societal-witnessed public miracle. Another rebuttal would be the building of a legend around an extraordinary natural phenomenon, especially if that population is physically or emotionally compromised, such as a recently emancipated enslaved population. This could be countered by the required condition of the argument for immediacy of recording and detailing, and of the national uniformity of the particulars of the event, for subsequent generational transmission.

The religious message of a public miracle plays an important role in the Jewish faith. However, attacks and rebuttals of public miracle credibility as, for example, in the case of the Kuzari principle, will undoubtedly continue. Attacks are generally based on the supposition of alternate explanations for the alleged "miraculous" phenomenon and postulating a hypothetical scenario to replace the claimed miracle. The rebuttals countering these attacks generally point out non-compliance with the defined criteria required of the Kuzari principle. In the final analysis, the conviction of believers will rest on a probabilistic justification of authenticity of the miracle as against speculations of alternate scenarios.

Revelation—the Divine Communication

The specifics of the relationship between God and humans is patently quite different amongst the various religions. However, what is common to all of the monotheistic religions is a conviction that there is a supernatural creator who is not totally absent and detached from humanity, but has communicated to natural humankind. The reasoned convictions of the believer are a rational response to the questions that are formulated by scientific inquiry of the natural world. Different religions will, of course, offer their own rationality and explanation for reaching their respective convictions. But for all faiths, it is that belief that there is a Creator, which enables an intellectually satisfying response to be made to the questions raised by the science narrative. On the other hand, non-belief or atheism will need to be satisfied with explaining reality through the science narrative alone, an endeavor which, as we have discussed above, is incomplete and leaves the essential meaningful questions unanswered.

7

Addressing Atheism, Theism, and Science

The atheist regards the world as "that's that;"
the theist regards the world as "that's why."

—Author's Words

The Origins of Religion

SCIENCE—SOCIOLOGY, PSYCHOLOGY, AND EVOLUTIONARY biology—has produced a vast academic literature on studies of the origin of religion and the development of belief, morality, and ritual.[1] Science could, therefore, quite rationally frame religion within the context of a purely sociological and psychological human phenomenon, unrelated to the truth or reality of the existence of the supernatural God. These studies have suggested that organized religion was born in the Near East during the Paleolithic era some 11,000 years ago. Michael Shermer has postulated that religious beliefs were born as a result of the brain's propensity firstly to perceive patterns, even in phenomena which are random, and secondly, to ascribe an agent as the cause of these phenomena. He has called the pattern-seeking inclination of the brain "patternicity" and the agency seeking "agenticity." In the earliest humans, these two proclivities developed into forms of religion as a protection

---

1. Ayala, "Difference of Being Human," 9015–22. Bellah, *Religion in Human Evolution*. Boehm, *Moral Origins*. Jones, "Ritual Animal," 470–72. Shermer, *Believing Brain*. Wilson, *Social Conquest of Earth*.

against the threats from their natural environment. Ritualism with religious content, whether expressed in chanting, dancing, or praying, became the cement that molded communities together—first as social groups, which later became the foundation of organized religion.[2] The evolution of moral behavior that became incorporated into religious belief could similarly be traced to the need for greater social cohesion. This became necessary, for example, to improve hunting efficiency as a group or defense against opposing communities, as well as for other social benefits.[3] Group selection has been postulated to answer the mystery of the development of altruism in human society within the development of religion.[4]

The origin, history, and development of religious beliefs makes for intellectually stimulating sociological and psychological science. However, its observational and inferential methodology places its conclusions into a category which is somewhat different from those of the physical and biological sciences. The latter necessarily follow the dictates of the scientific method, demanding, amongst others, falsifiability and reproducibility. This strategy of knowledge development would be inappropriate to the sociology and psychology of the development of religion.

Why do modern humans subscribe to religious beliefs today? For many, religious observance may be because of tradition, cultural norms, indoctrination, community belonging, fear (especially of death), paternalistic protection, power and influence, stability, or the provision of structure to life. For others, religious faith may come from deep reflection and a dedicated search for truth and meaning; religious observance and practice would follow as a consequence. Finding that truth is not immediate and the divergent paths of belief and non-belief have, in modern times, largely been governed by science.

---

2. Jones, "Ritual Animal," 470–72.
3. Boehm, *Moral Origins*.
4. Ayala, "Difference of Being Human." Wilson, *Social Conquest of Earth*.

Atheism

Atheism is a philosophy that espouses the denial of the existence of any god or gods.[5] For the purpose of this volume, atheism will be confined to the disbelief in the existence of the monotheistic God of Christianity, Islam, and Judaism—the so-called "Abrahamic religions." Atheism is broadly divisible into positive and negative atheism. Positive atheism maintains that there is no evidence to believe that God exists. The negative atheist, also referred to as the agnostic, reserves judgment on the matter, maintaining that he or she is not convinced that there is sufficient evidence to prove either for or against the existence of the Deity. Because positive atheism relies on evidence establishing the non-existence of God, it is also referred to as evidentialist atheism. Theism, however, may be either evidentialist, based on evidence supporting belief, or non-evidentialist, based on faith alone—as discussed in chapter 1. What then is the evidence that atheists put forward to positively deny the existence of God?

Deductive Evidence

This argument focuses on challenges to the attributes of God which religious believers hold by—omnipotence, omniscience, and omni-benevolence—as discussed in chapter 5. All three of these attributes are subject to the criticism that they can be shown to be logically contradictory. Thus, the stone paradox attacks omnipotence—can God create a stone he cannot lift? His inability to either construct the stone, or lift it, would thus seem to defeat omnipotence. Similarly, omniscience and freewill could appear to be logically contradictory. If God is omniscient, his actions are already predetermined, and therefore he would be unable to respond to change. Human freewill would also seemingly be constrained by God's foreknowledge of the future actions of the individual. Omnibenevolence, likewise, is apparently contradicted by the abundant

---

5. Bullivant and Ruse, *Oxford Handbook of Atheism*. Dawkins, *God Delusion*. McCormick, "Atheism."

presence in the world of outwardly meaningless suffering and evil, further amplified by the Job paradox of the righteous who suffer and the wicked who live under apparent privilege. If these essential attributes of God are indeed logically flawed it would make the existence of God an impossibility.

Inductive Evidence

These are items of evidence that would render the existence of God improbable. They have been discussed in greater detail in chapter 5. First and foremost is the problem of evil—perhaps the dominant challenge to religious belief. Secondly, the human proclivity to over-detect and over-interpret religious symbolism in natural environmental phenomena. Thirdly, the advent of modern science and its ability to progressively reveal more and more provable natural explanations for the phenomena of the natural world, especially those natural events and occurrences on which humans relied on for their sustenance, or were feared as "supernatural" phenomena. Perhaps the most important naturalistic challenge to religion has been the science of evolutionary biology that provides a materialistic biological explanation to much of the questions of life itself—see chapter 3, see pgs. 48–54.

The Santa Claus Argument

One of the arguments utilized by atheism is the problem of justifying a belief in something that cannot be directly perceived to exist. Theists sometimes reverse the challenge to the atheist to prove God does not exist. However, the same logic could pertain to attempts to disprove the existence of other imaginary things, such as Santa Claus, an imaginary teapot in the sky on the other side of the sun, elves, unicorns, etc.

The Hidden God

One of the most important tests of religious faith has been the belief in an "invisible" deity, one whose presence is not directly perceived—the so-called *Deus absconditus*. The apparent "absence" of God is, itself, made into a challenge by non-believers. The argument questions why, if God wanted humans to believe in him, he does not make his presence known. If he loves mankind why not reveal himself as his followers have regularly entreated him to do.

Defending Theism

The items of evidence mentioned above form the basis for evidentialist atheism—the denial of the existence of God. However, these challenges to theism can be defended in a number of ways.

The Origins of Religion

As mentioned above, the scientific study of the origins and development of religious beliefs makes for interesting and stimulating science, but these studies do not address the question of the truth of the existence or non-existence of God or, in fact, any of the over 2,500 gods identified over the course of the history of human civilization.[6] Scientific studies of religion are valuable intellectual and scholarly pursuits in their own right, but are independent of the triple truth statement (Does God exist? Did God create the universe? Does God control and govern the universe?).

Deductive Evidence

The three attributes of God attacked by atheism—omnipotence, omniscience, and omni-benevolence—are human constructs of language created by the human mind in order to enable divine concepts to be intelligible to the human mind—as we discussed

---

6. Jordan, *Encyclopedia of Gods*.

in chapter 5, see pgs. 83, 85–87. The anthropomorphic fallacy is the error of utilizing the vehicle of human language to define the attributes of God. Anthropomorphic, i.e., the human language narrative, conveys a representative or metaphorical meaning to specific communication between God and humans. Examples include the use of anatomical metaphors, such as the "finger of God" or emotional metaphors such as the "anger of God." Similarly, the omni- attributes of God are employed to translate divine communication to humans in human terms. However, human language is amenable to being manipulated by humans, and this may well distort their meaning or render them irrational or incoherent. For example, the stone paradox discussed in chapter 5, see pg. 86, is used by the atheist to attempt to defeat omnipotence. It is a fallacy of language fusing together two separate conflicting questions—the construction of the stone, and the lifting of the stone, into a single question, thereby rendering the challenge meaningless. Similarly, the posited paradox of God's foreknowledge frustrating human free will is also not valid, as there is nothing in the attribute of omniscience that dictates that God's knowledge of the future determines my action. God's foreknowledge and my future action are two separate and independent entities.

These erroneous anthropomorphic challenges may be defeated in their generality, as discussed, by the concept of non-predicate theism—the belief that God resides in a context beyond the exposition of human language, but who does communicate to his human creation, of necessity, through human language.

Inductive Evidence

Three inductive arguments were discussed above:

1. The challenge of evil and suffering to omni-benevolence is undoubtedly the most difficult to defend. Theologians and philosophers throughout the ages have put forward defenses of God's omni-benevolence in view of the apparently

meaningless existence of evil seen in the world.[7] The soul-making theodicy defense of John Hick, the freewill theodicy of Alvin Plantinga, and the best of all possible worlds theodicy of Leibniz have been discussed in chapter 5, see pgs. 88–90.

2. Atheism's argument that religion is a result of the human propensity to religious belief, whether from past history of humankind or the present, fails to answer the relevant question—the question of the triple truth statement of the existence of God. This challenge is incompetent as it is an *ad hominem*[8] challenge rather than one directed at the proposition of God's existence.

3. The third challenge, that religion arose from the need to provide solace for what is feared, or comfort for what one is dependent on, again avoids responding to the triple truth question and, as with 2, is similarly an *ad hominem* fallacious challenge. Science does indeed supply naturalistic answers to the phenomena that were the substance of devout entreaties of past generations, but again, science does not seek to answer the truth question. By definition, science, the study of the material world, is not equipped to investigate the nonmaterial, supernatural world.

The Santa Claus Argument

Drawing a comparison between human fictional artifacts such as Santa Claus, elves, imaginary teacups, etc., and whether God exists or not, becomes a circular argument depending on one's starting point. The atheist's starting point is that God is the same human artifact as the elves and Santa Claus. The theist standpoint is that the elves and Santa Claus are purely human artifacts—the origin of

---

7. Leibniz, *Theodicy: Essays on the Goodness of God*. Plantinga, "God, Freedom and Evil," 75–96. Scott, *Pathways in Theodicy*.

8. The fallacy of the ad hominem argument employs a strategy of avoiding attacking the substance of the argument by diverting to attack the character or the motive of the individual making the argument.

which in all cases can clearly and unequivocally be traced to a human author of fiction. No such inception of God can be so traced other than purported vague observations of human proclivities to religious belief. The crucial distinction between the monotheistic God and the fictional artifactual gods is discussed below under the section 3, see pgs. 116–118, "Just one more God and other myths." Atheism is unable to provide any evidence to prove their argument that the concept of God is similarly a fictional artifact, as against the theist standpoint, God is the supernatural being who created the humans who created the mythical artifacts.

The Hidden God

In the monotheistic religions, God is, in fact, not totally hidden. He communicated directly at Sinai to the entire nation of Israel; he has communicated to his human prophets; and he has communicated to humanity through the holy Scriptures, as well as through the commentaries of sages throughout the centuries. The reason why he has otherwise chosen to be largely "hidden" is not something he has chosen to reveal to his creation, i.e., humans. One can speculate on reasons from a human perspective. One of these reasons could relate to the pivotal religious need for humans to possess freewill, i.e., to have the relatively unfettered ability to choose between good and evil, and reward and punishment, rather than being created to merely function as robotic automatons. Clearly freewill and human responsibility would be constrained if the authority figure were to be patently present.

The Challenges of the Atheist

Organized religion has, in modern times, come under increasing attack from atheists and atheistic organizations.[9] Many challenges to religious belief are searching, well ordered, coherent, and legitimate. Others, however, especially some emanating from the

9. "Is God Dead?"

missionizing so-called "new atheists" have been more aggressive and, on occasion, simply distasteful and offensive.[10] I have selected a sample of quotations from prominent atheists and offered responses to these challenges.

Religion as Indoctrination

> Religion is regarded by the common people as true, but otherwise as false, and by the rulers as useful.
>
> —Seneca (4–65 CE)[11]

> Religion is something left over from the infancy of our intelligence. It will fade away as we adopt reason and science as our guidelines
>
> —Bertrand Russell (1872–1970)[12]

> Science and religion aren't friends. One relies on truth; the other relies on hope and obfuscation. Trying to equate the two, or giving religion undue authority, does the world no good.
>
> —Jerry Coyne (1949–)[13]

> What really moves people to believe in God is not any intellectual argument at all. Most people believe in God because they had been taught from early infancy.
>
> —Bertrand Russell[14]

> Religion is the sigh of the oppressed creature, the heart of a heartless world, and the soul of soulless conditions. It is the opium of the people.
>
> —Karl Marx (1818–1883)[15]

10. Taylor, "New Atheists."
11. Miller, "Brief History of Disbelief."
12. Russell, "Letter (1958) to Mr Major," 41–42.
13. Coyne, "Science and Religion Aren't Friends."
14. Russell, *Why I am Not a Christian*, 8.
15. Marx, *Critique of Hegel*.

> Philosophy is questions that may never be answered. Religion is answers that may never be questioned.
>
> —Anonymous

It is undoubtedly true that religious bodies have, ever since the birth of religion itself, indoctrinated children through their schools, and adults through their houses of worship and similar institutions. The consequence has, to a wide extent, been a religious belief devoid of intellectual content, and an unquestioning and unwavering acceptance of dogma, which prohibits any probing or searching for answers. This argument, while it may largely be true, is not a challenge to the truth statement of the existence of God—it is a criticism that directs itself to institutions of religion and their activities, but not religious faith.

Religion From Fear

> Fear is the mother of all gods. Nature does all things spontaneously by herself without their meddling.
>
> —Lucretius (99–55 BCE)[16]

> Why should I fear death? If I am, then death is not. If death is, then I am not. Why should I fear that which can only exist when I do not? Long time men lay oppressed with slavish fear. Religious tyranny did domineer. At length the mighty one of Greece began to assert the liberty of man.
>
> —Epicurus (341–270 BCE)[16]

> Religion is based primarily upon fear. It is partly the terror of the unknown and partly the wish that you have a kind of elder brother who will stand by you in all your troubles and disputes. Fear of the mysterious, fear of defeat, fear of death. Fear is the parent of cruelty and therefore it is no wonder if cruelty and religion have gone hand-in-hand.
>
> —Bertrand Russell[17]

16. Miller, "A Brief History of Disbelief."
17. Russell, *Why I am Not a Christian*, 18.

If one goes back to the beginning we should find that ignorance and fear created the gods. That fancy enthusiasm and deceit adorned them. That weakness worships them.

—Paul Henry Thiry, Baron d' Holbach (1723–1789)[18]

Why should I spend half of my Sunday hearing about how I'm going to hell?

—Homer Simpson[18]

Studies of the origin and development of religions have shown that fear has been a potent force for religious belief and, in particular, the fear of death. In some religious communities there appears to be a negative correlation between religious faith and the fear of death.[19] Other studies have shown no difference between believers and non-believers.[20] The implications of these investigations are certainly of importance clinically for the management of the elderly and the terminally ill—albeit that their findings still remain inconclusive. With respect to the ontological question of the existence of God, as with the question of indoctrination, the issue of fear, and the fear of death, may well be a potent driver of religious belief. It is nevertheless not relevant to the question of the truth statement of the existence of God.

Just One More God and Other Myths

We are all atheists about most of the gods that humanity has ever believed in. Some of us just go one god further.

—Richard Dawkins[21]

. . . if I am to convey the right impression to the ordinary man in the street I think I ought to say that I am an Atheist, because when I say that I cannot prove that there is

18. Miller, "A Brief History of Disbelief."
19. Kahoe, "Fear of Death," 379–82.
20. Feifel, "Religious Conviction and Fear," 353–60.
21. Dawkins, *God Delusion*, 77.

not a God, I ought to add equally that I cannot prove that there are not the Homeric gods.

—Bertrand Russell[22]

If I were to suggest that between the Earth and Mars there is a china teapot revolving about the sun in an elliptical orbit, nobody would be able to disprove my assertion provided I were careful to add that the teapot is too small to be revealed even by our most powerful telescopes. But if I were to go on to say that, since my assertion cannot be disproved, it is an intolerable presumption on the part of human reason to doubt it, I should rightly be thought to be talking nonsense. If, however, the existence of such a teapot were affirmed in ancient books, taught as the sacred truth every Sunday, and instilled into the minds of children at school, hesitation to believe in its existence would become a mark of eccentricity and entitle the doubter to the attentions of the psychiatrist in an enlightened age or of the Inquisitor in an earlier.

—Bertrand Russell[23]

As mentioned above, humankind has throughout its history, and right up to the present time, worshiped over 2,500 gods.[24] The atheist challenge is that choosing the monotheistic Judeo-Christian-Islamic God, is simply a matter of singling one out of the thousands of gods which have existed throughout human history. In other words, does traditional monotheistic religion belong to the same kind of myth as that which gave rise to the other polytheistic gods, or to believing in elves, unicorns, and teacups orbiting in space? Some of the aspects why humans have invented religions with their attached gods have been discussed above. In all cases these polytheistic gods have been human artifacts, created by humans as either effigies of humans or animals, or combinations of the two forms. Natural objects such as the sun, moon, and stars,

22. Russell, "Letter (1958) to Mr Major," 41–42.
23. Rational Wiki, "Russell's Teapot."
24. Jordan, *Encyclopedia of Gods*.

or natural phenomena such as holy mountains, or combinations of natural and human forms, and even deceased ancestors in underdeveloped countries, have all taken their place in the pantheon of gods worshiped throughout history and up to the present. In all of these cases of polytheistic worship, socio-psychological themes underlie the origin of these venerations and objects of worship. Emulation of power and beauty, fear of natural calamities, reverence for deceased ancestors, who are believed to have ethereal control of this world, may all have played a part in the genesis of these religious beliefs. In all of them there is some component of sensory, usually visual, representation to direct worship. The recognition and worship of the monotheistic God is, however, conceptually radically different. The second commandment expressly forbids the making of any kind of physical representation of God (Exod 20:4). The making of any kind of pictorial imagery to indicate or suggest a physical appearance of God is a cardinal sin—especially in the Jewish and Islamic faiths, and to a varying extent amongst Christian denominations. The ideation of the invisible and non-physical monotheistic God is, therefore, diametrically different to the concept of the visible sensate polytheistic gods. The monotheistic God cannot be imagined or conceived of in any kind of physical form whatsoever, and this supernaturalism categorizes God within a reality beyond the limits of human cognition—fundamentally different to all polytheistic belief systems. The same response would, of course, apply to the artifactual myths created by fictional authors, such as elves, gnomes, toothfairies, and orbiting teacups.

The Evils of Religion

The challenge of the presence of evil and needless suffering so prevalent in the world, and the theological defense of God's omnibenevolence, i.e., divine theodicy,[25] has been discussed above and in chapter 5, see pgs. 87–90. The purpose of theodicy is to respond to the accusation that God does not exist because there is so much

25. Theodicy is the defense of God's benevolence in the face of perceived evil and ostensibly needless suffering on Earth.

pointless evil and suffering. If God did exist, and is omnipotent, he should be empowered to prevent or ameliorate evil and suffering. If he is omni-benevolent, he would wish to prevent it. If he is omniscient, he would know about pointless suffering. Three other, somewhat different, challenges also relate to evil in religion—evil as a direct result of religious practices, evil practiced in the name of religion, and the evil which is produced from extracting only selected texts from the Bible.

Evil Perpetrated in the Name of Religion

> The most detestable wickedness, the most horrid cruelties and the greatest miseries that have afflicted the human race, have had their origin in this thing called religion.
>
> —Thomas Paine (1737–1809) [26]

> A tyrant must put on the appearance of uncommon devotion to religion. Subjects are less apprehensive of illegal treatment from a ruler whom they consider God fearing and pious. On the other hand they do less easily move against him, wrongly believing that he has had the gods on his side.
>
> —Aristotle (384–322 BCE) [27]

> You find this curious fact that the more intense has been the religion of any period and the more profound has been the dogmatic belief, the greater has been the cruelty and the worse has been the state of affairs. In the so-called ages of faith, when men really did believe the Christian religion in all its completeness, there was the Inquisition, with all its tortures; there were millions of unfortunate women burned as witches; and there was every kind of cruelty practiced upon all sorts of people in the name of religion.
>
> —Bertrand Russell[28]

26. Paine, *Age of Reason*, 165.
27. Feifel, "Religious Conviction," 353–60.
28. Russell, *Why I am Not a Christian*, 16.

Through the ages, violence, tyranny, cruelty, and religion have been bedfellows. The emotional power of religious faith is so strong that mixing it with political motives produces an incendiary mixture, which has been responsible, partly or wholly, for most of the conflicts of history.[29] Right up until the end of the second decade of the twenty-first century, much of the bloodshed and terrorism remains religiously-driven. Human tyrants and dictators have exploited human faith for their nefarious ends. (While it is certainly true that most of the wars of human history have been driven through exploitation of religion, the most violent genocidal massacres of the twentieth century, the Nazi Holocaust, the Stalinist purges, the Cambodian genocide, and the Rwandan holocaust, were, in fact, not religiously driven.) Does this indisputable fact of human history undermine religious faith, and the belief in the ultimate goodness and benevolence of the creator, who religious followers are commanded to emulate? The American social reformer, Susan B. Anthony (1829–1906) has articulated a brief response, albeit to a different challenge—that of chauvinism posing as religious direction:

> The religious persecution of the ages has been done under what was claimed to be the command of God. I distrust those people who know so well what God wants them to do to their fellows, because it always coincides with their own desires.
>
> —Susan B Anthony[30]

It is undoubtedly true that some of the most heinous crimes of history have been perpetrated by the most wicked of humans, masquerading as religious zealots. However, it is clear that the exploitation of religion by evil humans, whether for power or for wealth, is independent of the fundamental question of faith—does God exist or not?

---

29. Sacks, *Not in God's Name*.
30. Anthony, *A Defense of Elizabeth Cady*, 263.

Evil Consequent on Religious Practices

Extremist religious practices do clash with the health of individuals and communities. Many examples of preventable deaths in children and adults, due to religiously-based refusal of medical treatment, have been published in the medical literature.[31] In some cases, reliance has been on faith healing alone. In other cases medical treatment is simply refused if it is perceived to clash with a religious edict, such as, for example, blood transfusion.[32] Vaccine preventable outbreaks of diseases of major public health concern have not infrequently been the direct result of religiously motivated refusal to vaccinate.[33]

The challenge of evil due to religious observance, as with the atheist challenges of religion from fear, religion from indoctrination, and religiously-based atrocities, is one which is directed at human practices, or human interpretations of religion, and, again, are examples of ad hominem attack. They are not challenges on the fundamental truth question of the existence of God.

Evil from Biblical Literalism

> It is from the Bible that man has learned cruelty, rapine and murder, for the belief in a cruel God makes a cruel man and the Bible is a history of wickedness and has served to corrupt and brutalize mankind.
>
> —Thomas Paine[34]

> The God of the Old Testament is arguably the most unpleasant character in all fiction: jealous and proud of it; a petty, unjust, unforgiving control-freak; a vindictive, bloodthirsty ethnic cleanser; a misogynistic, homophobic, racist, infanticidal, genocidal, filicidal, pestilential,

---

31. Asser and Swan, "Child Fatalities," 625–29.
32. Rignes and Heystad, "Refusal of Blood Transfusion," 1672–87.
33. Riaz and Waheed, "Islam and Polio," 791–92. Stein-Zamir et al., "Measles Outbreaks," 207–14.
34. Paine, *Age of Reason*, 16, 166.

megalomaniacal, sadomasochistic, capriciously malevolent bully.

—Richard Dawkins[35]

A popular atheist weapon attacking religion comes from reveling in tales of horror and cruelty by excerpting selected texts from the Bible. Passages taken out of the Bible without explanation or context are gleefully used as ammunition by atheists to attack religion. For example, the massacres of the Amalekites in 1 Sam 15:3 or the Midianites in Num 31:1–18; the death penalty for the man picking up sticks on the Sabbath in Num 15:32–34; and the death penalty for homosexuality in Lev 20:13. In the Jewish religion, God has communicated his laws to humans in two structures of equal authority. The written law, or Torah, which is comprised of the five books of Moses, i.e., the initial five books of the Bible, contain only 79,847 words in total. It is, in reality, a brief précis of the religious jurisprudence of the Jews. Secondly, on an equal standing of authority is the Oral Torah, given directly by God to Moses, and passed down verbally from Moses to the elders, and then uninterruptedly from generation to generation up until the present. It was never meant to be written down, but because of the fear of it being lost during the various persecutions of the Jews, it was committed to writing in approximately 200 CE as the Mishnah. The explanations and comprehension of the Oral Law have been conveyed from sages and scholars to their students throughout the generations up to the present. The Mishnah consists of 63 tractates or chapters, almost all of which were followed by more extensive explanations and expansions in the Gemara, some 300 years later. The Mishnah and the Gemara form the Talmud of which there is a Babylonian and an Israeli version. The Babylonian Talmud, the more commonly studied, is some 5,422 pages long. It can be seen that the Oral Torah is vastly more extensive than the Written Torah. Thus, the true meaning of the excerpted passages from the Bible that were quoted above is elucidated in the Oral Torah. These explanations and discussions are vast, and well beyond the scope

35. Dawkins, *God Delusion*. 51.

of this book. Suffice it to say that severe punishments, such as the death penalty for various misdemeanors, were very seldom if ever carried out because of the stringency of the legal requirements for conviction. For example, the perpetrator would need to have been warned beforehand of the severity of the contemplated sin, and would have to provide assurances that he or she understood the implications. In addition, two unrelated reliable witnesses (who were themselves bounded by their own stringent qualifications) would have to testify to have personally witnessed the misdemeanor. Because of these very severe limitations for qualifications for witnesses and evidence, in some instances the death penalty was never carried out at all—for example, the rebellious son in Deut 21:18. The commentaries on the Talmud explain that they appear in the written Torah to convey a warning of the severity of these transgressions. Many qualifications were put in place before the death penalty would be carried out, thereby ensuring that execution was very rare indeed. The structure of the law was geared to acquit not to convict.[36]

Argumentum ad Hominem

What is apparent in much of the atheist challenges of religion is the fallacy of the *ad hominem* argument. The fundamental question is that of the basic triple truth statement whether God exists. Maintaining that believers are brainwashed, infantile, intellectually challenged, evil tyrants, or the subjects of evil tyrants, are incompetent diversionary responses to the fundamental question, and needlessly put believers on the defensive.

Atheism and Theism

The convictions of both atheists and theists are generally deeply entrenched. The materialism of atheism is founded on the belief that the natural world is decipherable through scientific investigation

36. B. Sanhedrin 32a, 34a.

alone—much of it by present science, and the remainder by the science of the future. Supernatural entities lie beyond science and therefore have no validity. Theism on the other hand conceives of an ontology beyond the natural, which is not reachable by science. The existence of the creator of nature, by logical inference, must be beyond nature itself. Finally, the persona of the creator cannot be comprehended by human cognition. What is known is what has been revealed by the revelations of each of the three Abrahamic religions. Central to the Judaic tradition is the historic fact that the revelation was a public one. It is historic, because it was a public and national revelation, which was passed down through generations uninterruptedly, directly from Sinai to the present. Theism insists that the world had to have been created and therefore had to have the creator. On the other hand Bertrand Russell has encapsulated the atheistic view:

> There is no reason to suppose that the world had a beginning at all. The idea that things must have a beginning is really due to the poverty of our imagination.[37]

This viewpoint implies no beginning, no inception, no driving force, and, *ipso facto,* no purpose and no meaning.

---

37. Russell, *Why I am Not a Christian*, 4.

8

Epilogue

Science frames the questions:
Revelation provides the answers.

—Author's Words

Questions from Science

WITH THE BIRTH OF the modern era of science, ushered in by Galileo and his telescope, more and more of the natural phenomena that had daunted earlier generations became less and less opaque. What lay behind plagues, droughts, floods, and earthquakes became more understandable as purely physical phenomena which could be measured, analyzed, and, in many cases, even predicted. Nevertheless, with the maturity of today's scientific enterprise, science can look back on itself and realize that it may well not be able to provide all the naturalistic answers it had once hoped for. A meta-scientific appraisal of the progress of science reveals what I have previously described as a Sisyphean pattern. Success in reaching milestones only reveals more investigational milestones further down the highway, in a seemingly unending journey of discovery. In some directions the highway ends in a cul-de-sac, where human science can proceed no further; for example, the cosmic horizon of some 42 billion light years away.

Science has indeed answered much. It has also shown us that as sophisticated and intricate as its tools may be, there are nevertheless questions it cannot address, and we need to look outside science for those answers. Whether searching for truth through science or religion, certainty is an unreachable goal. Certainty as defined by Cartesian epistemology[1] cannot be achieved.[2]

> It is difficult to define knowledge, difficult to decide whether we have any knowledge, and difficult, even if it is conceded that we sometimes have knowledge to discover whether we can ever know that we have knowledge in this or that particular case. . . . We believe that some beliefs are true, and some false. This raises the problem of verifiability: are there any circumstances which can justifiably give us an unusual degree of certainty that such and such a belief is true?
>
> —Bertrand Russell[3]

> In reality, both religion and science are expressions of man's uncertainty. Perhaps the paradox is that certainty, whether it be in science or religion, is dangerous.
>
> —Robert Winston, physician scientist and
> TV broadcaster (1940–)

Undoubtedly most of life's important decisions are taken with some degree of uncertainty—career, marriage, residence, investments, etc. Does interpreting reality boil down to conjecture—the materialism of the atheist, as against the spirituality of religious faith? Science has served a duality of contrasting roles—it has been used to underwrite non-belief while, alternately, it can and ought to be used to support religious faith. However, humans, especially those in the scientific community, seem to demand a higher degree

---

1. Cartesian epistemology was put forward by the 17th century French philosopher René Descartes. It proposes that we can only know things for certain if all possible alternates have been eliminated. It has been found to be an unacceptably stringent requirement for knowledge, as possible alternatives can always be found or devised, as for example the well-worn five-minute teaser. We cannot know with certainty that the universe is not five minutes old, i.e., that the universe came into existence five minutes ago with everything, including human memory, already imprinted into our psyche.

2. Newman, "Descarte's Epistemology."

3. Russell, *Analysis of Mind*, 98.

of certainty when it comes to religious faith. The singular demand is for "evidence."

Evidence

The well-worn aphorism "absence of evidence is not evidence of absence"[4] is one which comes up frequently in the science-religion debate. However, having to utilize science and the scientific method in order to provide evidence of the existence of God is inappropriate. Science, which investigates nature and natural phenomena, is not equipped to examine supernatural phenomena. If evidence, in scientific terms, is not forthcoming, then evidence for extra-natural phenomena fall outside of science's interests and its capabilities. Science is a creation of humans—it is therefore logically inappropriate to utilize an entity created by humans to investigate the ontology of humans. For this enquiry other tools need to be utilized—those of philosophy and theology. Philosophy would employ the tools of reason, theology would examine the elements of revelation. Philosophy formulates the questions of reasoning which science does not answer to. The question of "meaning" and "why" are usually rejected by atheists as irrelevant, extraneous, and digressive. And yet as far back as some ten centuries ago, the Middle-Ages philosopher, Maimonides, sought answers beyond the naturalistic sciences of his time:

> For according to Aristotle who holds that the universe has not had a beginning, an ultimate final cause cannot be sought even for the various parts of the universe. Thus, it cannot be asked, according to his opinion, what is the final cause of the existence of the heavens? Why are they limited by this measure or by that number? What is matter of this description? What is the purpose of the existence of the species of animals or plants? . . . Natural philosophy investigates into the object of everything in nature, but it does not treat of the ultimate final cause.[5]

4. Altman and Martin, "Statistical Notes," 485.
5. Maimonides, *Guide for the Perplexed*, 3: 13, 272.

Dismissing questions of meaning represents a failure of atheism to address the pivotal question of reality. Essentially, it descends to a metaphysical nihilism. Bertrand Russell articulated this succinctly in a BBC radio debate in 1948:

> Some atheists agree that the universe is a brute fact. "The Universe just exists" they say "and that's that—it has no explanation at all."[6]

What science, in its most modern form, has contributed to religious belief is to demonstrate that the reality of the universe demands an explanation beyond the physical elements of which it is constituted. Science has taken us to a certain frontier of knowledge, and in doing so has framed the questions that need to be responded to. Atheism will stop at this point and trust that knowledge frontiers, even those of the natural world, will be breached by future science, and what cannot be breached, such as the ultimate cosmic horizon (of 42 billion light years away), is irrelevant. Religion recognizes that there is a finitude to man's scientific discovery; and further enquiry requires investigation by tools other than science. Religion recognizes the existence of a supernatural being beyond the confines of scientifically demonstrable nature who was responsible for creating that nature. Revelation identifies that supernatural creator. It also defines a purpose and a meaning to nature rather than simply accepting the "brute fact" that the "universe just exists" and "that's that."

Science Frames the Questions

The Universe

The sciences, such as particle physics, cosmology, evolutionary biology, and molecular genetics, have revealed a universe of staggering complexity and astonishing beauty. Scientists who have a genuine love for their vocation, cannot be but overawed by what is unveiled by scientific discovery. Even those of a not particularly

---

6. "Fr. Copleston vs. Bertrand Russell."

religious inclination, from Darwin (see chapter 2, pg. 31) to Einstein, have expressed their veneration of the natural world:

> If something is in me which can be called religious then it is the unbounded admiration for a structure of the world so far as our science can reveal it.
>
> —Albert Einstein in a letter to an atheist in 1954[7]

The beauty and the complexity of the universe is, of course, interpretable dualistically. The non-believer will often recognize, appreciate and be "overwhelmed with a feeding of awe" but will suppress the need to acknowledge the Creator because of science.

> We, all of us, share a kind of religious reverence for the beauties of the universe, for the complexity of life. For the sheer magnitude of the cosmos, the sheer magnitude of geological time. And it's tempting to translate that feeling of awe and worship into a desire to worship some particular thing, a person, an agent. You want to attribute it to a maker, to a creator. What science has now achieved is an emancipation from that impulse to attribute these things to a creator.
>
> —Richard Dawkins[8]

However, science is not the instrument that reveals how that beauty and complexity came about. Bertrand Russell has taken one view of the universe, just being a "brute fact," that it simply exists and "that's that." However, deeper reflection would demand a more searching inquiry than simply accepting the universe, with its vast complexity, as a "brute fact—and nothing more."

Science, by definition, is an empirical endeavor. It cannot be subjective—the scientific method dictates its objectivity. It is therefore inappropriate to utilize science to validate beauty, or to use science to explicate the more elemental source of beauty.

---

7. See Einstein, "Letter to an Atheist," 43.
8. Dawkins, "God Delusion Debate."

The Diversity of Life

Chapter 3 describes the enormous complexity of living organisms on the planet, with close on two million species existing in the world today—representing approximately 10 percent of life which ever existed on earth. Evolution biology is founded on the understanding that species evolve as a result of competitive advantage resulting from random mutational or other diversifying genetic events. The newly evolved species would out-compete its competitors in that ecosystem and establish itself to replace the originating species. Can this enormous biological diversity and intricate synchrony of living organisms be solely explicable on a materialistic explanation of mutational events and natural selection?

Biological Drives

Science has very elegantly, and even with a degree of disarming simplicity, elucidated Darwinian evolution. The mechanics of evolution, however, depend on the existence of fundamental biological drives—essentially drives which ensure the preservation of advantageous genes, and often in conflict with the urge to self-preservation. In chapter 3, see pgs. 53–54, the question was raised whether the powerful and universal biological drives of sex and parenting are solely a natural result of the physical phenomenon of selective advantage. Alternately, could the biological drives, so intrinsic to the engine that powers evolution, convey a deeper and more profound teleological message? The direct inference is that these drives may well have been a strategy built into the evolutionary process by its creator.

Fine-tuning of the Universe

In chapter 3, see pgs. 60–65, the exquisitely precise parameters which specify the existence of the universe were discussed, as well as the meticulously exact parameters which allowed for human life—the fine tuning of the universe and the anthropic principle.

EPILOGUE

Again, the responses are dualistic. The non-belief response to fine-tuning has been to put forward the multiverse hypothesis.[9] This hypothesis speculates, with little evidence to support it, that there exists not only our own universe but many other universes, if not an infinite number. Our universe, which happens to be so finely tuned for life, just happens to be the one in which we live and are conscious of, and are able to describe. The multiverse hypothesis has been criticized for lacking scientific supporting evidence.[10] Until some supporting, scientifically valid evidence should eventuate, the multiverse hypothesis must remain as the non-believer's pipe dream. Occam's Razor also requires a more direct and simpler answer.

Meta-science

Chapter 2 discussed the Sisyphean personality of meta-science—the observation that scientific discovery follows a pattern of discovery and elucidation of specific questions which, themselves, generate additional and often logarithmically more questions to be investigated by future science. Many materialists are confident that ultimately there will be a scientific capability of addressing all the relevant questions of the natural world. Similar optimism of the ultimate power of science pertained at the start of the twentieth century, as described above in chapter 3. As previously discussed, the history of the scientific endeavor does not support this confidence.

The Frontiers of Knowledge

Over and above the progress of knowledge, there will always remain frontiers that cannot be breached. One example was the cosmic horizon of 42 billion light years away. Beyond that horizon is a reality which humankind can never know. Then there are also the questions that arise on which science can only speculate. For

---

9. Adler, *Ultimate Guide*, 42–47.
10. Ellis, "Does the Multiverse Really Exist," 38–43.

example, the common chestnut of what preceded the Big Bang that gave birth to our universe. Various hypotheses have been advanced, such as quantum tunneling, where extremely small subatomic particles appear in different places and times.[11] It is postulated that one of these, several billion times smaller than an atom, may have expanded some 13.7 billion years ago into the entire universe of hundreds of billions of galaxies. Alternatively, as Stephen Hawking has offered:

> . . . one could say 'the boundary conditions of the universe is that it has no boundary'. The universe would be completely self-contained and not affected by anything outside itself. It would neither be created nor destroyed. It would just BE.[12]

On the issue of the Creation itself, Hawking further speculates:

> The initial rate of expansion also would have had to be chosen very precisely for the rate of expansion still to be so close to the critical rate needed to avoid re-collapse. This means that the initial state of the universe must have been very carefully chosen indeed if the hot big bang model was correct right back to the beginning of time. It would be very difficult to explain why the universe should have begun and just this way, except as the act of a God who intended to create beings like us.[13]

Science can content itself with the uncertainty of the no-boundary universe of Hawking. Conversely, religion would also need to content itself with the uncertainty of why the creator would create a universe of such magnitude and diversity, when only a small fraction would be available to human knowledge, given that humans are the religious center of the creation.

---

11. Hellemans, "Escape from the Nucleus," 26–27.
12. Hawking, *Brief History of Time*, 155.
13. Hawking, *Brief History of Time*, 144.

EPILOGUE

The Regularity, Orderliness, and Harmony of the Universe

The regularity, intricacy, and synchronicity, together with the formidable complexity of all the myriads of components of the universe, and all of this built from a mere seventeen elemental building blocks, is cogent suggestion of purposeful conception rather than uncaused consequentialism of undirected but propitious chance.

Revelation Provides Answers

Revelation, as a more generic term in religion, refers to communication by God to humans, and is an integral component of all religious faiths. (The term "Revelation" when capitalized has a specific meaning in the Christian religion, referring to the last book of the Christian Bible.) In chapter 6, revelation was discussed as it applied to the Jewish religion—God's direct communication at Sinai to the entire nation of Israel. It was here where the law was transmitted to the prophet Moses, and then passed on from generation to generation in an uninterrupted chain to the present. The effort required to embark on studying God's revelation to humans is one of the cardinal freewill requirements in the Jewish faith. As mentioned in chapter 6, in the Jewish religion the daily prayers incorporate a portion from the Talmud that puts the study of Torah ahead of all the other commandments. Its importance is that humans are enjoined to make the freewill choice to comprehend the message communicated from God to man. Thereby, humankind would understand that there is a Creator who created and controls the world. To grasp and comprehend the communication between God and humankind is a universal requirement of all religions, albeit each within their own specific doctrine.

The existential questions such as: "why are we here?" and "what purpose is there to life?" can only but be avoided by the materialist, who is epistemically bounded by scientific investigation and scientific knowledge. Science raises these questions; but science cannot supply these answers. Responses to these questions of purpose, meaning, and guidance can proceed along one of four paths.

1. Polytheism and Related Ideologies

Mythical beings have been conceived, created, and authored by humans and worshiped by other humans, i.e., the gods of the ancients and other related myths. They served a societal need for comfort, societal cohesion, and objects for supplications and entreaties. They also provided an imagined supernaturalism to answer the ontological questions arising from considerations of natural phenomena.

2. Atheism and Scientism

This is the response of rejecting the need to provide an answer to these questions. In this view, the scientific endeavor itself more than amply and naturally provides its own beauty, wonderment, and admiration of the universe, without the need to postulate anything supernaturally.

3. Non-evidential Theism and Fideism

This response is one of uncompromised recognition and faith that the supernal creation is a work of the supernatural Creator, the monotheistic God. This view posits a purer and ostensibly more genuine conviction and sincere faith, undiluted, unaffected, and untainted by evidence manufactured by humans.

4. Science-aided Evidential Theism

Science is recognized as a supreme divine gift to purposefully aid and strengthen the faith of modern humankind. Deep reflection on the nature of the scientific endeavor contributes the foundation of the conviction of the religious scientist. To the scientist-theist, it is religious faith which completes the circle of the searching questions that are generated by science and scientific knowledge.

Defending Theism: the Scientific Narrative

Does theism need defending? From population studies, as described in the introduction—it undoubtedly does. Religion is declining sharply in most western countries. The main hatchet being used to bury religion is science—the mantra being that science does, or will, explain everything. Looking for any supernatural explanation of reality is not only needless, naïve, or even childlike, or, at best, intellectually impoverished. And yet it is, in fact, the very insights which science provides, which give support to the ideology of theism.

Theism is, thus, defensible in two steps.—

1. By Inference to the Best Explanation

Abductive reasoning shows that there is a greater plausibility of the existence of the creator of the universe than the reasoning put forward by atheism for two reasons:

1. The insights from the grandeur of the universe supplied by the discoveries of science and the dynamic frontiers of scientific knowledge.

2. The greater plausibility of the existence of the creator when seeking to answer the questions of responsibility for the origin of the universe, the purpose of the universe, and the purpose of humankind. This, as against the vacuous "brute fact" and "that's that" responses of atheism.

2. Identity by Revelation

The conclusion of the circle of reality is recognizing the identity of the Creator via his communication to humankind through revelation by religion. Evidential theism—the theism best placed to defend itself against the challenges of atheism, depends on revelation for its final "proof."

The fundamental question rests on the truth of the existence of God. The atheist arguments of people's fears, needs, or other psychological motives of believers are irrelevant to that truth. Neither is the argument from theists of the moral benefits to society of religious belief, relevant to the ultimate question of truth. For this reason I have avoided discussion on the sociological benefits of organized religion—as important as I do think they are in the present era. The science narrative to defend theism is one which requires a response to the pivotal question—was the universe created by the Creator? Does the Creator control the universe? Consequently is humankind answerable to the Creator?

Many religious believers will trust their belief to be authentic in themselves and eschew the need for evidence—non-evidential theists. I will leave aside this subset of theists as there is obviously little dialogue between non-evidential theism and non-belief. Neither atheism nor theism can prove this truth with evidence, if evidence is confined to scientific evidence alone.

Atheism maintains that evidence for the non-existence of God is not necessary. If science is the sole arbiter of truth, it is not required to prove a negative, as it is similarly not obliged to do so with any other mythical item such as elves, unicorns, and orbiting teacups. Theism maintains that the requirement for scientific evidence is a tautological fallacy, as it requires humans to create evidence to prove the entity that created them. Thus, "evidence" for the theist cannot be scientific evidence. The "evidence" of the theist, as mentioned above, comes partly from what science reveals, i.e., the abductive reasoning of inference to the best explanation. However, this is only the halfway stop, and proof of the truth has to be substantiated by the revelation that lies outside the bounds of science. Without revelation, the "evidence" goes only part of the way to establishing truth. The revelations of different religions, while they are meaningful to their respective adherents, do nevertheless differ substantially from each other. *Inter alia*—in

EPILOGUE

the Christian religion it is the resurrection of Jesus; in the religion of Islam it is the direct revelation to the prophet Muhammad; in the Jewish religion it is the public revelation to the entire Jewish nation at Mount Sinai. In defending theism, the only truly satisfactory answer to the existential questions of the meaning of reality comes from the combination of both science plus revelation.

This book has been motivated by a need I felt personally as a professional scientist, to put forward a defense of theism from a scientific perspective. The intellectual quality of the atheism-theism dialogue is, unfortunately, often sullied, because it frequently deviates either to ad hominem attacks on the believer, or to lurid misinterpretations of biblical texts. The fundamental questions ought to be:

1. The truth of the existence of God and
2. The truth of God's revelation to humankind.

The ultimate consideration is whether the atheistic standpoint of materialism that the universe is explicable through the insights and knowledge from science alone, or the theistic standpoint that it is what science has revealed that confirms that there had to be a Creator.

In Conclusion

Science has undergone its own evolution. In the darkness of the prescientific era, religion provided comfort and reassurance amid the uncertainties and fears that the plagues and calamities of the natural world brought forth. The advent of scientific discovery and scientific application dispensed with much of human subservience to nature's challenges. But with the advance of the modern scientific era came a newfound confidence that the religion of yesteryear was no longer necessary. Science now provided that needed comfort and reassurance. Whatever challenges nature could confront humankind with, science would, if not now, at least in the future, be able to handle. There was no need to look for any supernatural phenomenon. The new age of science hubris supported the growth of non-belief.

I would posit that science may be evolving into a phase of what could be termed science maturity, which is now tempered with a modicum of sobriety. That being said, the admiration for the achievements of science is not, in any way, being dimmed, nor is the respect for the authenticity, precision, and validity of scientific findings being at all diminished. However, what is now emerging is a realization that science is not the master of all reality. A new appreciation of science is emerging, one that is conveying a cardinal message. The message that what science is now intimating is the need to recognize that beyond science there is a supernatural being, the creator of the creation that science is revealing and illuminating. Furthermore, science is showing us that it cannot fully define reality and it never will. That reality lies beyond the ever-expanding frontier of scientific knowledge. Science is now arriving at its most modern phase, the phase of science maturity. Outside of science's sphere of influence, it is religious revelation that completes the circle of the search for truth—the circle which science began with its own revelation of the wonders of the creation and is completed only by religious revelation.

> Seek the Lord while He can be found, call to Him while He is near.

—Isa 55:6

Bibliography

Adams, Robert M. "Predication, Truth and Transworld Identity in Leibniz." In *How Things Are*, edited by J. Bogen and J.E. McGuire, 235–82. Dordrecht: D. Reidel, 1984.
Adler, Robert. "The Ultimate Guide to the Multiverse." *New Scientist* 212 (2011) 42–47.
Aiello, Leslie C., and Peter Wheeler. "The Expensive Tissue Hypothesis." *Current Anthropology* 36 (1995) 199–221.
Alter, Torin. "The Knowledge Argument Against Physicalism." *Internet Encyclopedia of Philosophy*. https://www.iep.utm.edu/know-arg/.
Altman, Douglas G., and Bland J. Martin. "Statistical Notes: Absence of Evidence is not Evidence of Absence." *British Medical Journal* 311 (1995) 485.
Amesbury, Richard. "Fideism." https://plato.stanford.edu/entries/fideism/.
Ananthaswamy, Anil. *Through Two Doors at Once. The Elegant Experiment that Captures the Enigma of our Quantum Reality*. London: Random, 2018.
Anthony, Susan B. *A Defence of Elizabeth Cady Stanton Against a Motion to Repudiate her Woman's Bible*. Meeting of the National American Suffrage Association. HWS 4 (1902).
Appelson, Robert R. *Greenway and the Torah Blueprint for Creation*. www.jct.ac.il/sites/default/files/Bor_Hatora/Appelson%20BHT%2024%20final.pdf.
Armant, Robert St., and Thomas E. Horton. "Revisiting the Definition of Animal Tool Use." *Animal Behaviour* 75 (2008) 1199–1208.
Asser, Seth M., and Rita Swan. "Child Fatalities from Religion-Motivated Neglect." *Pediatrics* 101 (1998) 625–29.
ATLAS Collaboration. "Combined Search for the Standard Model Higgs Boson Using up to 4.9 fb–1 of pp Collision Data with the Atlas Detector at the LHC." *Physics Letters B* 710 (2012) 49–66.
Avery, Oswald T., et al. "Studies on the Chemical Nature of the Substance Inducing Transformation of Pneumococcal Types. Induction of Transformation by a Deoxyribonucleic Acid Fraction Isolated from Pneumococcus Type III." *Journal of Experimental Medicine* 79 (1944) 137–58.
Aviezer, Nathan. *In the Beginning: Biblical Creation and Science*. Brooklyn: Ktav, 1990.
Ayala, Francisco J. "The Difference of Being Human: Morality." *Proceedings of the National Academy of Sciences* 116 (2010) 9015–22.

BIBLIOGRAPHY

Barrow, John D. *The Anthropic Cosmological Principle.* Oxford: Oxford University Press, 1986.

———. "Cosmologies with Varying Light Speed." *Physical Review D* 59 (1999) 043515-22.

BBC. "The Bible Tops 'Most Influential' Book Survey." *BBC News,* November 21, 2014. https://www.bbc.com/news/entertainment-arts-30036581.

———. "'Virgin Mary' toast fetches $28,000." *BBC News,* November 23, 2004. http://news.bbc.co.uk/2/hi/4034787.stm.

Bellah, Robert Needly. *Religion in Human Evolution. From the Paleolithic to the Axial Age.* Boston: Harvard University Press, 2011.

Bergmann, Michael. "Skeptical Theism and Rowe's New Evidential Argument from Evil." *Nous* 35 (2001) 278-96.

Bevelacqua, Joseph. "Standard Model of Particle Physics—a Health Physics Perspective." *Health Physics* 99 (2010) 613-23.

Bingham, John. "Christianity at Risk of Dying Out in a Generation, Warns Lord Carey." *The Telegraph,* November 18, 2013. https://www.telegraph.co.uk/news/religion/10458380/Christianity-at-risk-of-dying-out-in-a-generation-warns-Lord-Carey.html

Bishop, John. *Believing by Faith:An Essay in the Epistemology and Ethics of Relgious Belief.* New York: Clarendon, 2007.

Boehm, Christopher. *Moral Origins. The Evolution of Virtue, Altruism and Shame.* New York: Basic, 2012.

Boon, Sarah. "21st Century Science Overload." blog.cdnsciencepub.com/21st-century-science-overload/.

Brooks, Michael, and Helen Phillips. "Beyond Belief. In Place of God." *New Scientist* 2578 (2006) 8-11.

Bullard, Gabe. "The World's Newest Major Religion: No religion." *National Geographic,* April 22, 2016. https://news.nationalgeographic.com/2016/04/160422-atheism-agnostic-secular-nones-rising-religion/.

Bullivant, Stephen. "Europe'sYoung Adults and Religion. Findings from the European Social Survey (2014-2016) to Inform the 2018 Synod of Bishops." Benedict XVI Centre for Religion and Society. London: St. Mary's University, 2018.

Bullivant, Stephen, and Michael Ruse. *The Oxford Handbook of Atheism.* Oxford: Oxford University Press, 2013.

Byrgen, Lars O. "Intergenerational Health Responses to Adverse and Enriched Environments." *Annual Review of Public Health* 34 (2013) 49-60.

Capaccioni, F., et al. "The organic-rich surface of comet 67P/Churyumov-Gerasimenko as seen by VIRTIS/Rosetta." *Science* 347 (2015) 628-1-628-4.

Carter, Brandon. "Large Number Coincidences and the Anthropic Principle in Cosmology." In *Confrontation of Cosmological Theories with Observational Data,* 291-98. Krakow: Dordrecht D. Reidel, 1974.

Castelvecchi, David. "Quantum Puzzle Baffles Physicists." *Nature* 561 (2018) 446-47.

Chofetz Chaim. *The Blueprint of Creation.* New York: Feldheim, 1990.

BIBLIOGRAPHY

Clifford, William K. *The Ethics of Belief*. www.memelyceum.com/documents/ethics_of_belief.pdf.
Cohen, Mitchell L. "Changing Patterns in Infectious Disease." *Nature* 406 (2000) 762–67.
Collins, Francis S. *The Language of God: A Scientist Presents Evidence for Belief*. London: Pocket, 2007.
Copeland, Edmund, et al. "Dynamics of Dark Energy." *International Journal of Modern Physics* 15 (2006) 1753–1935.
Corey, Michael A. *The God Hypothesis. Discovering Design in our Just Right Goldilocks Universe*. Plymouth: Rowman & Littlefield, 2001.
Courvoisier, Thierry J.-L., and Ian Robson. "The Quasar 3C 273." *Scientific American* 264 (1991(50–57.
Coyne, Jerry A. "Science and Religion Aren't Friends." *USA Today*, October 11, 2010. https://usatoday30.usatoday.com/news/opinion/forum/2010-10-11-column11_ST_N.htm
———. *Why Evolution is True*. Oxford: Oxford University Press, 2010.
Craig, William Lane. *The Kalam Cosmological Argument*. Eugene, OR: Wipf & Stock, 2000.
Daeschler, Edward B., Neil H. Shubin, and Farish A. Jenkins. "A Devonian Tetrapod-Like Fish and the Evolution of the Tetrapod Body Plan." *Nature* 440 (2006) 757–63.
Darwin, Charles. *The Descent of Man*. London: John Murray, 1871. www.ataun.net/bibliotecagratuita/Classics%20in%20English/Charles%20Darwin/The%20Descent%20of%20Man.pdf
———.*The Origin of Species*. London: John Murray, 1859. darwin-online.org.uk/converted/pdf/1861_OriginNY_F382.pdf
Davies, Brian. *An Introduction to the Philosophy of Religion*. Oxford: University of Oxford Press, 2004.
Davies, Paul. *The Goldilocks Enigma: Why is the Universe Just Right for Life?* New York: Mariner, 2006.
Dawkins, Richard. *The Blind Watchmaker*. New York: W.W. Norton, 1986.
———. *The God Delusion*. London: Bantam, 2006.
———. "The God Delusion Debate. Richard Dawkins vs John Lennox." http://www.protorah.com/wp-content/uploads/2015/01/The-God-Delusion-Debate-Full-Transcript.pdf.
———. *The Greatest Show on Earth. The Evidence for Evolution*. London: Black Swan, 2010.
———. "Is Science a Religion?" *The Humanist* (1997) 26–29.
———. *The Selfish Gene*. Oxford: Oxford University Press, 1989.
De Buhr, Hendrik, and Robert Jan Lebbink. "CRISPR to Combat Viral Infections." *Current Opinion in Immunology* 54 (2018) 123–29.
Desai, Jay, and Kiarash Sadrieh. "It's Time to Remember Hippocrates." *Journal of Child Neurology* 33 (2018) 501–2.
Dine, Michael, and Alexander Kusenko. "Origin of the Matter-Antimatter Asymmetry." *Reviews of Modern Physics* 76 (2004) 1–30.

Dodd, Matthew S., et al. "Evidence for Early Life in Earth's Oldest Hydrothermal Vent Precipitates." *Nature* 543 (2017) 60–64.

Dor, Yuval, and Howard Cedar. "Principles of DNA Methylation." *The Lancet* 392 (2018) 777–86.

Doudna, Jennifer A., and Emmanuelle Charpentier. "The New Frontier of Genome Engineering with CRISPR-Cas9." *Science* 346 (2014).

Einstein, Albert. "Letter to an Atheist (1954)." In *Albert Einstein: The Human Side*, edited by Helen Dukas and Banesh Hoffman, Princeton: Princeton University Press, 1979.

Ellis, George. "Does the Multiverse Really Exist?" *Scientific American* 305 (2011) 38–43.

Ellis, George, and Joe Silk. "Defend the Integrity of Physics." *Nature* 516 (2014) 321–23.

Endler, John A. "Some General Comments on the Evolution and Design of Animal Communication Systems." *Philosophical Transactions of the Royal Society B* 340 (1993) 215–25.

Evans, C. Stephen. *Faith Beyond Reason: A Kierkegaardian Account*. Grand Rapids: Eerdmans, 1998.

Falk, Dean. "Evolution of Brain and Culture; the Neurological and Cognitive Journey from Australopithecus to Albert Einstein." *Journal of Anthropological Sciences* 94 (2016) 99–111.

Feifel, Herman. "Religious Conviction and Fear of Death Among the Healthy and the Terminally Ill." *Journal for the Scientific Study of Religion* 33 (1974) 353–60.

Finocchiaro, Maurice A. *Galileo on the World Systems*. Berkeley: University of California Press, 1997.

Flintoff, Louisa. "Identical Twins: Epigenetics Makes the Difference." *Nature Reviews Genetics* 6 (2005) 667.

"Fr. Copleston vs. Bertrand Russell: The Famous 1948 BBC Radio Debate on the Existence of God." www.biblicalcatholic.com/apologetics/p20.htm.

Frackowiak, Richard. *Human Brain Function*. London: Academic, 2004.

Francois, Bernard, et al. "The Lourdes Medical Cures." *Journal of the History of Medicine and Allied Sciences* 69 (2014) 135–62.

Gallup. "In U.S., 42 percent Believe Creationist View of Human Origins." *Gallup*, June 2, 2014. https://news.gallup.com/poll/170822/believe-creationist-view-human-origins.aspx.

Galtung, Johan. "On the Social Costs of Modernization. Social Disintegration, Atomie/Anomie and Social Development." *Development and Change* 27 (1996) 379–413.

Gardner, Martin. "The Religious Views of Stephen J Gould and Charles Darwin." *The Skeptical Inquirer* 23 (1999) 8–13.

Gibbons, Ann. "Turning Back the Clock: Slowing the Pace of Prehistory." *Science* 338 (2012) 189–91.

Gleiser, Marcelo. *The Island of Knowledge*. New York: Basic, 2014.

BIBLIOGRAPHY

Goldhahn, Jorg, et al. "Could Artificial Intelligence Make Doctors Obsolete?" *British Medical Journal* 363 (2018) 1–3.

Gottlieb, Dovid. "Living Up to the Truth. The Controversy." https://ohr.edu/explore_judaism/living_up_to_the_truth/the_controversy/1011.

———. "The Kuzari Principle—Introduction." https://www.dovidgottlieb.com/comments/Kuzari_Principle_Intro.htm.

Gould, Stephen J. "Non-overlapping Magisteria." *Skeptical Enquirer* 23 (1999).

Gribbin, John. *Schrodingers Kittens, and the Search for Reality. Solving the Quantum Mysteries.* Boston: Little Brown, 1995.

Griffith, Frederick. "The Significance of Pneumococcal Types." *Journal of Hygiene* 27 (1928) 113–59.

Guth, Alan H. *The Inflationary Universe.* New York: Basic, 1997.

HaLevi, Yehuda. *The Kuzari.* Translated by N. Daniel Korobkin. New York: Feldheim, 2013.

Hancock, Angela M., et al. "Human Adaptations to Diet, Subsistence, and Ecoregion are Due to Subtle Shifts in Allele Frequencies." *Proceedings of the National Academy of Sciences* 107 (Suppl 2) (2010) 8924–30.

Hand, Eric. "Mars Rover Finds Long-Chain Organic Compounds." *Science* 347 (2015) 1402–3.

Hatfield, Gary. "Rene Descartes." https://plato.stanford.edu/archives/sum2018/entries/descartes/.

Hawking, Stephen. *A Brief History of Time.* London: Bantam, 2016.

Heijmans, Bastiaan T., et al. "Persistent Epigenetic Differences Associated with Prenatal Exposure to Famine in Humans." *Proceedings of the National Academy of Sciences* 105 (2008) 17046–49.

Hellemans, Alexander. "Escape from the Nucleus. Ionization via Quantum Tunneling Observed." *Scientific American* 296 (2007) 26–27.

Herculano-Houzel, Suzana. "The Remarkable, Yet not Extraordinary Human Brain as a Scaled Up Primate Brain and its Associated Cost." *Proceedings of the National Academy of Sciences* 109 (Suppl 1) (2012) 10661–68.

Hershey, Alfred D., and Martha Chase. "Independent functions of viral protein and nucleic acid in growth of bacteriophage." *Journal of General Physiology* 36 (1952) 39–56.

Heschel, Abraham Joshua. *God in Search of Man.* Cleveland: Meridian, 1955.

Hick, John H. *Philosophy of Religion.* Belmont, CA: Wadsworth Cengage Learning, 2007.

Horodecki, Ryszard, et al. "Quantum Entanglement." *Reviews of Modern Physics* 81 (2009) 865–42.

"How did "credibile est, quia ineptum est" become "credo quia absurdum"?" https://christianity.stackexchange.com/questions/27855/how-did-credibile-est-quia-ineptum-est-become-credo-quia-absurdum.

Hoyle, Fred. "The Universe: Past and Present Reflections." *Annual Review of Astronomy and Astrophysics* 20 (1982) 1–36.

Hume, David. "Dialogues Concerning Natural Religion." In *An Introduction to the Philosophy of Religion*, edited by Brian Davies, 63. Oxford: Oxford University Press, 2004.

———. "An Enquiry Concerning Human Understanding." In *An Introduction to the Philosophy of Religion*, edited by Brian Davies, 23. Oxford: Oxford University Press, 2004.

Hume, David, and L. A. Selby-Bigge. *An Enquiry Concerning Human Understanding Section X Miracles*. http://www.gutenberg.org/files/9662/9662-h/9662-h.htm.

International Human Genome Sequencing Consortium. "Initial sequencing and analysis of the human genome." *Nature* 409 (2001) 860–921.

"Is God Dead?" *Time Magazine*, April 8, 1966.

Jackson, Frank. "What Mary Didn't Know." *Journal of Philosophy* 83 (1986) 291–95.

Jaganathan, Deepa, et al. "CRISPR for Crop Improvement. An Update Review." *Frontiers in Plant Science* (2018) 1–17.

James, William. *The Will to Believe*. https://www.mnsu.edu/philosophy/THEWILLTOBELIEVEbyJames.pdf.

Jankowiak, Tim. "Immanuel Kant." *Internet Encyclopedia of Philosophy*. https://www.iep.utm.edu/kantview/

Jones, Dan. "The Ritual Animal." *Nature* 493 (2013) 470–72.

Jordan, Michael. *Encyclopedia of Gods: Over 2500 Deities of the World*. London: Kyle Cathie, 2002.

Jorgenson, Lyric A., et al. "The BRAIN Initiative: Developing Technology to Catalyse Neuroscience Discovery." *Philosophical Transactions of the Royal Society of London B. Biological Sciences* 370 (2015) 1–12.

Joyce, Gerald F. "The Antiquity of RNA-Based Evolution." *Nature* 418 (2002) 214–21.

Kahoe, Richard D. "The Fear of Death and Religious Attitudes and Behaviour." *Journal for the Scientific Study of Religion* 14 (1975) 379–82.

Kaplan, Aryeh. *Maimonides' Principles. The Fundamentals of Jewish Faith*. New York: NCSY, 1984.

Kierkegaard, Soren. *Fear and Trembling*. https://www.solargeneral.org/wp-content/uploads/library/fear-and-trembling-johannes-de-silentio.pdf.

Kim, Eric S., and Tyler J. VanderWeele. "Mediators of the Association Between Religious Service Attendance and Mortality." *American Journal of Epidemiology* 188 (2019) 96–101.

Klug, Aaron. "Rosalind Franklin and the Discovery of the Structure of DNA." *Nature* 219 (1968) 808–10.

Kragh, Helga, and Robert Smith. "Who Discovered the Expanding Universe?" *History of Science* 41 (2003) 141–62.

Krause, Lawrence M. *A Universe from Nothing*. New York: Free, 2012.

Kun, Adam, et al. "The Dynamics of the RNA World." *Annals of the New York Academy of Sciences* 1341 (2015) 75–95.

Laplane, Lucie, et al. "Why Science Needs Philosophy." *Proceedings of the National Academy of Sciences of the USA* 116 (2019) 3948–52.

Larson, Edward J., and Larry Witham. "Leading Scientists Still Reject God." *Nature* 394 (1998) 313.

BIBLIOGRAPHY

Lemaitre, George. "Evolution of the Expanding Universe." *Proceedings of the National Academy of Sciences* 20 (1934) 12–17.

Leibniz, Gottfried Wilhelm. "Theodicy." In *God and the Problem of Evil*, edited by William L Rowe, 218–36. Oxford: Blackwell, 2001.

———. *Theodicy: Essays on the Goodness of God, the Freedom of Man and the Origin of Evil*. Dumfries and Galloway: Anodus, 2017.

Lichtenstein, Aharon. "The Source of Faith is Faith Itself." *Tradition* 47 (2015) 188–91.

Luzzatto, Moshe Chaim. *Da'at Tevunot (The Knowing Heart)* 122. https://www.sefaria.org/Da'at_Tevunoth.122?lang=bi&with=all&lang2=en.

———. *The Way of God*. Translated by Aryeh Kaplan. New York: Feldheim, 1998.

Lyko F., et al. «The Honey Bee Epigenomes: Differential Methylation of Brain DNA in Queens and Workers." *PLOS Biology* 9 (2001) 1–12.

The Maharal. "Tiferet Yisrael". Translated and Commentary by Ramon Widmonte. Jerusalem: Urim, 2016.

Maimonides. *The Guide for the Perplexed* Translated by M. Friedlander. New York: Routledge & Sons, 1936.

———. *Yesodei HaTorah*. https://www.chabad.org/library/article_cdo/aid/904960/jewish/Yesodei-haTorah-Chapter-One.htm.

Marx, Karl. *Critique of Hegel's Philosophy of Right*; Translated by Joseph O' Malley. 1970. https://www.marxists.org/archive/marx/works/download/Marx_Critique_of_Hegels_Philosophy_of_Right.pdf

Maslin, Keith T. *An Introduction to the Philosophy of the Mind*. Cambridge: Polity, 2007.

McCormick, Matt. "Atheism." *Internet Encyclopedia of Philosophy*. https://www.iep.utm.edu/atheism/.

McDonald, William. "Soren Kierkegaard." https://plato.stanford.edu/archives/win2017/entries/kierkegaard/.

McInerney, Ralph, and John O'Callaghan. "Saint Thomas Aquinas." https://plato.stanford.edu/archives/sum2018/entries/aquinas/.

McIver, Tom. "Ancient Tales and Space-Age Myths of Creationist Evangelism." *The Skeptical Inquirer* 10 (1986) 258–76.

Melamed, Yitzhak Y., and Martin Lin. "Principal of Sufficient Reason." https://plato.stanford.edu/archives/spr2018/entries/sufficient-reason/.

Mendl, Michael, et al. "An Integrative and Functional Framework for the Study of Animal Emotion and Mood." *Proceedings of the Royal Society B* 277 (2010) 2895–2904.

Milem, Bruce. "Four Theories of Negative Theology." *The Heythrop Journal* 48 (2007) 187–204.

Miller, Jonathan. "A Brief History of Disbelief." https://www.youtube.com/watch?v=Ad_fTX8rEKs&t=46s.

Miller, Kenneth R. *Finding Darwin's God*. New York: Harper Perennial, 2007.

Miller, Stanley L., and Harold C. Urey. "Organic Compound Synthesis on the Primitive Earth." *Science* 130 (1959) 245–51.

Mostafavi, Hakhamanesh, et al. "Identifying Genetic Variants that Affect Viability in Large Cohorts." *PLoS biology* 15 (2017) 1–29.
The National Academy of Sciences. *Science, Evolution and Creationism.* https://www.nap.edu/read/11876/chapter/1#iii.
National Academies of Sciences, Engineering, and Medicine. *Reproducibility and Replicability in Science.* Washington, DC: The National Academies Press, 2019.
Nielsen, Kai. "Wittgensteinian Fideism." *Philosophy* 42 (1967) 191–209.
Navarrete, Ana, et al. "Energetics and the Evolution of Human Brain Size." *Nature* 480 (2011) 91–93.
Newman, Lex. "Descartes' Epistemology." https://plato.stanford.edu/archives/win2016/entries/descartes-epistemology.
Niemitz, Carsten. "The Evolution of the Upright Position." *Die Naturwissenschaften* 97 (2010) 241–63.
Oparin, Aleksandr. *The Origin of Life.* New York: Dover, 1936.
Paine, Thomas. *The Age of Reason.* 1807. https://www.globalgreybooks.com/content/books/ebooks/age-of-reason.pdf.
Pennisi, Elizabeth. "The Burden of Being a Biped." *Science* 336 (2012) 974.
Pennock, Robert T. "The Argument from Ignorance and the Limits of Methodological Naturalism." In *Scientists Confront Creationism and Intelligent Design*, edited by Andrew Petto and Laurie Godfrey, 309–38. New York: W. W. Norton, 2007.
Perakh, Mark. "Confronted with Critique, Schroeder Lost Voice." https://pandasthumb.org/archives/2005/11/confronted-with.html.
———. "The End of the Beginning, Prof Aviezer Interprets the Book of Genesis." www.talkreason.org/articles/aviezer.cfm.
Pew Research Center. "Public Views on Human Evolution." http://www.pewforum.org/2013/12/30/publics-views-on-human-evolution/.
———. "What is Each Country's Second Largest Religious Group?" http://www.pewresearch.org/fact-tank/2015/06/22/what-is-each-countrys-second-largest-religious-group/.
Plantinga, Alvin. "The Free Will Defense." In *Philosophy of Religion: An Anthology* edited by Michael Peterson, et al., 167–86. New York: Oxford University Press, 1971.
———. "God, Freedom and Evil." *International Journal for Philosophy of Religion* 12 (1981) 75–96.
———. "Is Belief in God Properly Basic?" *Nous* 15 (1981) 41–51.
———. *The Nature of Necessity.* Oxford: Clarendon, 1974.
Plato. *Euthyphro.* www.indiana.edu/~p374/Euthyphro.pdf.
Polkinghorne, John C. *Science and Religion: In Quest of Truth.* London: Society for Promoting Christian Knowledge, 2011.
Popper, Karl. *Conjectures and Refutations.* London: Routledge Classics, 1963.
Pritchard, Duncan. "Wittgensteinian Quasi-Fideism." *Oxford Studies in the Philosophy of Religion* 4 (2011) 145–59.

BIBLIOGRAPHY

Pritchard, Jonathan K., et al. "The Genetics of Human Adaptation: Hard Sweeps, Soft Sweeps and Polygenic Adaptation." *Current Biology* 20 (2010) R208–15.
Qu, Hsueh. "Doxastic Involuntarism." *Mind* 126 (2017) 53–92.
Rational Wiki. "Non-Overlapping Magisteria." https://rationalwiki.org/wiki/Non-Overlapping_Magisteria.
———. "Russel's Teapot." https://rationalwiki.org/wiki/Russell%27s_Teapot. November 24, 2018.
Rees, Martin. *Just Six Numbers: The Deep Forces that Shape the Universe*. London: Orion, 1999.
Reinhuber, Thomas. "Deus Absconditus/Deus Revelatus." https://referenceworks.brillonline.com/entries/religion-past-and-present/deus-absconditusdeus-revelatus-SIM_03572.
Riaz, Fatima, and Yasir Waheed. "Islam and Polio." *The Lancet Infectious Diseases* 14 (2014) 791–92.
Rignes, Hege K., and Harald Heystad. "Refusal of Blood Transfusions Among Jehovah's Witnesses." *Journal of Religion and Health* 55 (2016) 1672–87.
Roberts, Alice. *Evolution. The Human Story*. London: DK, 2011.
Rowe, William L. *Philosophy of Religion: An Introduction*. Belmont, CA: Wadsworth Cengage Learning, 2007.
Rubin, Vera. "Dark Matter in the Universe." *Scientific American* 9 (1998) 106–10.
Russell, Bertrand. *The Analysis of Mind*. 1922. https://archive.org/details/analysisofmind032971mbp/page/n75.
———. "Letter (1958) to Mr Major." In *Dear Bertrand Russell: A Selection of his Correspondence with the General Public 1950–1968*, 41–42. London: Allen & Unwin, 1969.
———. *Why I am not a Christian*. 1957. https://www.academia.edu/11791682/Bertrand_Russell_-_Why_I_Am_Not_a_Christian_and_Other_Essays_on_Religion_and_Related_Subjects.
Sacks, Jonathan. *Not in God's Name*. New York: Schocken, 2015.
———. *The Great Partnership*. London: Hodder and Stoughton, 2011.
Sadler, Greg. "Anselm of Canterbury (1033-1109)." *Internet Encyclopedia of Philosophy*. https://www.iep.utm.edu/anselm/.
Scherman, Nosson, ed. *The Complete Artscroll Siddur*. New York: Mesorah, 1984.
Schiller, Martin R. "The Mini-Motif Synthesis Hypothesis for the Origin of Life." *Journal of Translational Science* (2016) 289–96.
Schlick, Moritz. "Meaning and Verification." *The Philosophical Review* 45 (1936) 339–69. http://www.ifac.univ-nantes.fr/IMG/pdf/Schlick_Meaning_Verif.pdf.
Schroeder, Gerald. *Genesis and the Big Bang*. New York: Bantam, 1990.
Scott, Mark. *Pathways in Theodicy: An Introduction to the Problem of Evil*. Minneapolis: Fortress, 2015.

BIBLIOGRAPHY

Searle, John. "Theory of Mind and Darwin's Legacy." *Proceedings of the National Academy of Sciences* 110 (Suppl 2) (2013) 10343–48.

Seeskin, Kenneth. "Maimonides." https://plato.stanford.edu/archives/spr2017/entries/maimonides/.

Shermer, Michael. *The Believing Brain. From Ghosts and Gods to Politics and Conspiracies*. London: Constable and Robinson, 2011.

Singh, Vijai, et al. "Exploring the Potential of Genome Editing CRISPR-Cas9 Technology." *Gene* 599 (2017) 1–18.

Slipher, Vesto. "Nebulae." *Proceedings of the American Philosophical Society* 56 (1917) 403–9.

Smoot, George F. "The Cosmic Background Explorer (COBE). Results." In *Perspectives in High Energy Physics and Cosmology*, edited by Antonio Gonzalez-Arroyo and Cayetano Lopez, 136–47. Madrid: World Scientific, 1992.

Soloveitchik, Joseph B. *Halachic Man*. Philadelphia: The Jewish Publication Society, 1983.

———. *The Lonely Man of Faith*. New York: Doubleday, 1965.

"Soul Has Weight Physician Thinks." *The New York Times*, March 11, 1907. https://www.nytimes.com/1907/03/11/archives/soul-has-weight-physician-thinks-dr-macdougall-of-haverhill-tells.html.

Sparke, Linda S., and John S. Gallagher. *Galaxies in the Universe*. Cambridge: Cambridge University Press, 2007.

Spelberg, Brad. "Dr. William H. Stewart: Mistaken or Malignant?" *Clinical Infectious Diseases* 47 (2008) 294.

Spiro, Ken. *Crash Course in Jewish History*. New York: Targum, 2011.

Steffen, Will, et al. "The Anthropocene: Are Humans Now Overwhelming the Great Forces of Nature." *Journal of the Human Environment* 38 (2007) 614–21.

Stein-Zamir, C., et al. "Measles Outbreaks Affecting Children in Jewish Ultra-Orthodox Communities in Jerusalem." *Epidemiology and Infection* 136 (2008) 207–14.

Steinberg, Milton. "The believer in God has to account for the existence of unjust suffering." https://www.azquotes.com/quote/1412494.

Stoljar, Daniel. "Physicalism." https://plato.stanford.edu/archives/win2017/entries/physicalism/.

Striedter, Georg F., et al. "Brain and Behavior." *Proceedings of the National Academy of Sciences* 109 (Suppl 1) (2012) 10607–11.

Sutter, Paul M. *Your Place in the Universe: Understanding our Big Messy Existence*. New York: Prometheus, 2018.

Swift, Art. "Is US Belief in Creationist View of Humans at New Low?" *Gallup*, May 22, 2017. https://news.gallup.com/poll/210956/belief-creationist-view-humans-new-low.aspx.

Swinburne, Richard. *The Existence of God*. Oxford: Oxford University Press, 2004.

———. *Is there a God?* Oxford: Oxford University Press, 1996.

BIBLIOGRAPHY

Tanner, Larry. "Definitively Refuting the Kuzari Principle." larrytanner. blogspot.com/2010/07/definitively-refuting-kuzari-principle.html.

Taylor, James E. "The New Atheists." *Internet Encyclopedia of Philosophy.* https://www.iep.utm.edu/n-atheis/.

Turing, Alan M. "Computing Machinery and Intelligence." *Mind* 49 (1950) 433–60.

Turner, Michael S. "Origin of the Universe." *Scientific American* 22 (2009) 36–43.

Van Elk, Michael, et al. "Priming of Supernatural Agent Concepts and Agent Detection." *Religion, Brain and Behaviour* 6 (2014) 4–33.

Van Horn, John D., et al. "Mapping Connectivity Damage in the Case of Phineas Gage." *PLoS One* 7 (2012) 1–24.

Venter, John Craig, et al. "The Sequence of the Human Genome." *Science* 291 (2001) 1304–51.

Walsh, Anthony. "Ideology in Physics: Ontological Naturalism and Theism Confront the Big Bang, Cosmic FineTuning, and the Multiverse of M-Theory." *Journal of Ideology* 39 (2009) 1–17.

Warwick, Kevin, and Huma Shoch. "Passing the Turing Test Does Not Mean the End of Humanity." *Cognitive Computation* 8 (2016) 409–19.

Watson, James Dewey, and Harry Compton Crick. "Molecular Structure of Nucleic Acid." *Nature* 171 (1953) 737–38.

Wilson, Edward O. *The Social Conquest of Earth.* New York: Liveright (Norton), 2012.

Wilson, Robert W. "The Cosmic Microwave Background Radiation." *Reviews of Modern Physics* (1979) 433–49.

Wikipedia. "Hilbert's Paradox of the Grand Hotel." https://en.wikipedia.org/wiki/Hilbert%27s_paradox_of_the_Grand_Hotel.

———. "Infinity." https://en.wikipedia.org/wiki/Infinity.

———. "Our Lady of the Underpass." https://en.wikipedia.org/wiki/Our_Lady_of_the_Underpass.

———. "Texas Sharpshooter Fallacy." https://en.wikipedia.org/wiki/Texas_sharpshooter_fallacy.

Wikiquote. "Epicurus." https://en.wikiquote.org/wiki/Epicurus.

Wittgenstein, Ludwig. *Philosophical Investigations.* Translated by G.E.M. Anscombe. London: Wiley-Blackwell, 2009.

———. *Tractatus Logico-Philosophicus.* Translated by D. F. Pears and B. F. McGuiness. London: Routledge Classics, 2001.

Wood, Bernard, and Terry Harrison. "The Evolutionary Context of the First Hominins." *Nature* 470 (2011) 347–52.

Wray, Kevin. *An Introduction to String Theory.* https://math.berkeley.edu/~kwray/papers/string_theory.pdf.

Author Index

Anaximander, 15
Anselm, 17
Anthony, Susan B, 120
Aquinas, Thomas, 13, 17, 90
Archbihop of Canterbury, 5
Aristotle 66, 119, 127
Avery, Oswald, 36
Aviezer, Nathan, 32

Barrow, John, 63
Bishop, John, 21
Braun, Wernher von, 44

Carter, Brandon, 63
Chase, Martha, 37
Clifford, WK, 20
Copernicus, Nicolaus, 66
Coyne, Jerry, 6, 114
Craig, William Lane, 14, 15
Crick, Francis, 37, 42

Darwin, Charles, 31, 31n10, 35-36, 48, 53, 67, 69, 129
Dawkins, Richard, 30n8, 53, 116, 121-122, 129
Descartes, René, 73, 126n1

Einstein, Albert, 1, 54, 57, 129
Ellis, George, 64, 131
Epicurus, 87, 115
Evans, C Stephen, 21

Franklin, Rosalind, 37

Galilei, Galileo, 66, 125
Gleiser, Marcelo, 24, 34
Gottlieb, Rabbi Dovid, 103-104
Griffith, Frederick, 36-37
Guth, Alan, 56

Haldane, JBS, 49
Hawking, Stephen, 61n44, 132
Hershey, Alfred, 37
Heschel, Abraham Joshua, 28
Hick, John H, 88-89, 112
Hilbert, David, 15n16
Holbach, Paul Henry Thiry, Baron d', 116
Hoyle, Fred, 44, 55
Hubble, Edwin, 55
Hume, David, 12, 14, 16, 100, 101, 102
Huxley, Thomas H, 71

Jackson, Frank, 75, 76
James, William, 20

Kant, Immanuel, 14, 17
Kelvin, Lord, 45, 45n3
Kierkegaard, Soren, 19, 20

Lamarck, Jean-Baptiste, 35
Leibniz, Gottfried Wilhelm, 14, 88, 112

Lemaitre, George, 54-55
Lichtenstein, Aharon, 23
Lucretius, 115
Luzzatto, R' Moshe Chaim, 94

MacLeod, Colin, 36
Maimonides, xi, 11, 14, 23, 24, 90, 91, 92, 96, 127
Marx, Karl, 114
McCarty, Maclyn, 36
Mendel, Gregor Johann, 36, 40
Miller, Stanley, 49-50

Oparin, Aleksandr, 49
Owen, Richard, 71

Paine, Thomas, 119, 121
Paley, William, 16, 44
Pascal, Blaise, 19-20
Penzias, Arno, 55
Plantinga, Alvin, 17-18, 21, 88, 89, 112
Pseudo-Dionysius, 90
Ptolemy, 66

Rees, Martin, 60
Rowe, William L, 88
Russell, Bertrand, ix, 46n7, 114, 115, 117, 119, 124, 126, 128, 129

Schrodinger, Erwin, 59
Schroeder, Gerald, 32
Searle, John, 75
Seneca, 114
Shermer, Michael, 106
Sigerist, Henry, 45
Slipher, Vesto, 54
Soloveitchik, Joseph B, 23
Steinberg, Milton, 88
Stewart, William H, 45
Swinburne, Richard, 17, 64

Tertullian, 19
Tippler, Frank, 63
Turing, Alan, 75

Urey, Harold, 49-50

Watson, James, 37, 42
Wilson, Robert, 55
Winston, Robert, 126
Wittgenstein, Ludwig, 19, 20, 53, 79, 85, 98

Yehuda HaNasi, 97
Yehudah HaLevi, 23, 102

Subject Index

a priori argument, 17
abiogenesis, 33, 49-50
Abrahamic monotheistic religions, 80, 108, 124
Accountability, 84, 86
ad hominem argument, 112, 112n8, 121, 123, 137
age of the earth, 52
age of the universe, 52, 55
agenticity, 106
agnostic, 108
always, 15, 84
Amalekites, 87, 122
American Association for the Advancement of Science (AAAS), 5
Anaximander, 15
Andromeda, 57
Animal breeders, 51
Anselm, 17
Anthony, Susan B, 120
Anthropic, 9, 60, 63, 66
    anthropic principle, 62-65, 67, 130
    strong anthropic principle, 63
    weak anthropic principle, 63
Anthropocene, 68, 78
Anthropomorphic, xi, 9, 79, 80, 81, 82, 83, 92, 93, 111
    anthropomorphic attributes, 81, 82, 83, 92
    anthropomorphic fallacies, xi, 9, 92, 93, 111

anthropomorphic predication, 93
antimatter, 60
apophatic theology, xi, 90
Aquinas, Thomas, 13, 17, 90
arational belief systems, 21
Archbihop of Canterbury, 5
argument by analogy, 16-17, 44-45
argument from probability, 17
arguments from causation, 13-14
arguments from contingency, 13-14
arguments from degrees, 13-14
arguments from motion, 13-14
Aristotle, 66, 119, 127
artificial intelligence, 34, 75
artificial selection, 51
astronomical unit, 56
atheism, 2, 4, 9, 10, 12, 53, 88, 95, 104, 108, 109, 110, 112, 113, 123, 128, 134, 135, 136, 137
atheism, definition, 108
atheism evidential, 108, 110
atheism, negative, 108
atheism positive, 108
atheim-theism debate, 2, 9, 45, 46n7, 90, 128, 137
atheist, x, xi, 2, 6, 29 ,30, 31, 43, 53, 88, 90, 106, 108-124, 126, 127, 136, 137
atomic model, 46
atrocities, 121

153

SUBJECT INDEX

attributes, xi, 9, 10, 79, 80, 81, 83, 86, 87, 88, 90, 91, 92, 108, 109, 110, 111
attributions, 22, 81, 82, 83, 92
Australopithecus, 70, 71
Avery, Oswald; MacLeod, Colin; and McCarty, Maclyn, 36
Aviezer, Nathan, 32

Barrow, John and Tippler, Frank, 63
benefitting society, 2
best of all possible worlds theodicy, 89-90, 112
biblical literalism, 9, 121-123
Big Bang, 15, 55, 58, 61, 61n44, 132
Big Crunch, 61
Biogenesis, 50-51
Biogeography, 52
biological drive, 53-54, 130
bipedalism, 69-70
Bishop, John, 21
Black Hole, 58, 62
Bosons, 47, 48
Brain, human, 48, 70, 71-72, 75
brain size, 70, 71-72
Braun, Wernher von, 44
breath of life, 67
brute fact, 46, 46n7, 128, 129, 135

carbon, 63
Carter, Brandon, 63
Cartesian dualism, 73
Cartesian epistemology, 126, 126n1
cat-in-the-box, 59
centrality of humans, 66, 67, 68
cerebral cortex, 72, 74
certainty, 126-127, 126n1
Chinese room experiment, 75
Christianity, 5, 19, 82, 99, 105
circle of truth, 135, 138
classical philosophical arguments, 13-18
Clifford, WK, 20
cognitive functions, 5, 7, 23, 71, 72

comets, organic material, 50
common ancestry of life, 35, 52
Commonality of biochemistry, 52
communication, divine, 9, 10, 79, 80, 81. 82, 83, 92, 94-105
concealment, divine, 11-13
consciousness, 71, 74, 76-77
conviction, 22, 46, 49, 91, 94, 99, 104, 123, 134
Copernicus, Nicolaus, 66
cosmic horizon, 25, 57, 64, 125, 128, 131
cosmic microwave background, 55, 56
cosmological argument, 13-15
Cosmology, 15, 18, 54-65, 67, 128
Coyne, Jerry, 6, 114
Craig, William Lane, 14, 15
credibility, 102, 104
CRISPR-Cas9, 38

dark energy, 58-59
dark matter, 58-59
Darwin, Charles, 31, 31n10, 35-36, 48, 53, 67, 69, 129
Darwinian evolution, 16, 35-36, 39, 45, 71, 130
Dawkins, Richard, 30n8, 53, 116, 121-122, 129
death penalty, 122-123
Deductive evidence, 108-109, 110-111
Defending theism, 110-113, 135-137
Descartes, René, 73, 126n1
Descriptive/observational inquiry, 25
design argument, 16, 17, 18, 44-65, 67
design as purpose, 16-17
design as regularity, 17
Deus Absconditus, 13, 83, 110
direct communication, 82-83, 96, 133
disconfirm, 90n17

SUBJECT INDEX

diversity of life, 31, 130
divine gift, 3, 9, 134
Divine simplicity, 84-85
DNA, 33, 36-42, 50, 78
    DNA copying, 50
    DNA sequencing, 38-39
doctrines, 6, 24, 95, 133
dogma, 66-68, 115, 119
dominion, 67
double slit experiment, 59
doxastic involuntarism, 20, 20n28
dualism, Cartesian, 73, 74, 82
dualist theory of mind, 73
Dutch hunger study, 40-41

Einstein, Albert, 1, 54, 57, 129
    Einstein general and special relativity, 54, 57
electromagnetic, 46, 47, 55, 59, 61, 64
electrons, 46, 47, 55, 56, 59
elementary particles, 45, 46-48
Ellis, George, 64, 131
emotional, 22, 104, 111, 120
encephalization, 70-71
Epicurus, 87, 115
epidemiological studies, 2-3, 25
epigenetics, 39-42
    epigenetic regulation, 41
    epigenome, 41, 42
essence of God, 7, 11, 13, 84, 85, 91
Euthyphro dilemma, 86-87, 86n9
Evans, C Stephen, 21
Evidence, x, 3, 7, 8, 20, 21, 23, 31, 108, 110, 113, 127-128, 134, 136
    evidence deductive, 108-109, 110-111
    evidence inductive, 109, 111-112
    evidence of miracles, 101
    evidence scientific, 7, 18, 26, 28, 36, 48, 50, 51, 53, 55, 64, 65, 67, 69, 127, 131, 136

evidential atheism, 108, 110
evidential theism, 7, 134; non-evidential theism 108
evidentialism, 21
evil, religious challenges, 87-90, 92, 109, 111-112, 113, 123
    Evils consequent on religion, 121
    Evils from biblical literalism, 121-123
    Evils in name of religion, 119-120
    Evils of religion, 118-119
evolutionary biology, 16, 18, 29, 35-36, 39, 45, 48, 51-53, 106, 109, 128, see also "biogenesis"
evolution of humankind, 29, 48, 68, 69-71, 77-78
evolutionary medicine, 48, 48n11
evolution theology, 53-54
existentialist, 17, 76, 81-82, 133, 137
expanding universe, 54-56
expensive-tissue hypothesis, 70-71
experimental, 25, 26, 27, 36, 49, 50, 55, 64
exploitation of religion, 120
eye, 16

fabricated myth, 102-103
fallacies, 86, 92, 93, 100, 111, 112n8, 123, 136
false prophet, 99
falsifiability, 25, 52, 107
fear and religion, 107, 109, 112, 115-116, 118, 121, 136, 137
fermions, 46-47
fictional artefacts, 112
fideism, 19-22, 134
fine tuning, 17, 60-64, 130-131
first cause, 13
force particles, 47
foreknowledge, 86, 108, 111

SUBJECT INDEX

fossils, 50,52
Franklin, Rosalind, 37
freewill, 12, 18, 85, 89. 108, 112, 113, 133
free-will theodicy, 89, 112
friends, science and religion aren't, 6, 114
frontier of knowledge, xi, 7, 8, 25, 36, 37, 38, 39, 40, 43, 44, 47, 50, 54, 60, 72, 108, 131-132. 135, 138
fundamental forces, 45, 46, 47, 48, 55, 61

Gage, Phineas, 74-75
Galapagos, 52
Galaxies, 54, 56, 57-58, 61-62, 132
Galilei, Galileo, 66, 125
Gallup poll, 29.
Gemara, 97, 99, 122
genetic code, 33, 36-39
    gene editing, 38
    genetic diversity, 51
genocidal conflicts, 2, 120,
geocentric, 66
Gleiser, Marcelo, 24, 34
gluon, 47
God of the gaps, 5, 7, 32-33
Goldilocks, 62, 63
Gottlieb, Rabbi Dovid, 103-104
gravitational force, 46, 47, 58-59, 61, 61n44
greater good, 89-90
Greek philosophy, 22
Griffith, Frederick, 36-37
Guth, Alan, 56

Halacha, 22
Haldane, JBS, 49
Hawking, Stephen, 61n44, 132
heliocentric, 66
heredity, 35-43
heritable reproduction, 35

Hershey, Alfred and Chase, Martha, 37
Heschel, Abraham Joshua, 28
Hick, John H, 88-89, 112
Higgs boson, 25, 48
Hilbert, David, 15n16
Hilbert's thought experiment, 15, 15n16
histone tails, 41
Holbach, Paul Henry Thiry, Baron d', 116
holocaust, 89, 120
Holy Scriptures, 22, 67, 76, 83, 85, 96, 113,
Hominins, 69, 69n8
    Homo erectus, 70
    Homo habilis, 70, 71
    Homo sapiens, 57, 70, 72, 81
horizon of knowledge, 7, 8, 25, 34, 39, 42, 57, 64, 125, 128, 131
Hoyle, Fred 44, 55
Hubble, Edwin, 55
    Hubble space telescope, 54
    Hubble's law, 54, 55
    Hubble deep field, 57
hubris, xi, 8, 138
    human evolution, 29, 48, 68, 69-71, 77-78
    human brain, 48, 70, 71-72, 75
    human genome, 38, 39-40, 42
    Human Genome Project, 39-40, 42
    human mind, 24, 71, 72-75, 77, 84, 110
humanism, 3, 5
Hume, David, 12, 14, 16, 100, 101, 102
Huxley, Thomas H, 71

image of God, 67
immutability, divine, 84
Impenetrability, divine, 83-84
incendiary mixture, 2, 120
individuality, 76

SUBJECT INDEX

indivisibility, 84, 85
indoctrination, 107, 114-115, 116, 121
Inductive evidence, 109, 111-112
Inference to the best explanation, 25, 135, 136
infinity, 13, 15, 15n16, 25, 65, 84
inflation, cosmic, 56
influential book, 48, 67
intelligence, human, 69, 77, 85, 114
intentional purpose, 18
interpretations, 6, 9, 63, 85, 98, 121
invisible deity, 81, 110, 118
irreconcilable doctrines, 6
Islam, 82, 99, 108, 137

Jackson, Frank, 75, 76
James, William, 20
Jesus, 99, 137
Job, 87, 92
Job paradox, 109
Journal of Evolutionary Medicine, 48n11
Judaism, 22, 23, 82, 95, 99, 102, 108
junk genes, 40

Kalam, 13
Kant, Immanuel, 14, 17
Kelvin, Lord, 45, 45n3
Kierkegaard, Soren, 19, 20
know God, 11, 12, 13, 18, 21, 24, 81, 83, 92, 94
knowledge argument, 76
knowledge frontier, xi, 7, 8, 25, 34, 35, 38, 39, 40, 42, 43, 47, 50, 54, 60, 128, 131-132, 135, 138
Kuzari, 23, 102-104
Kuzari principle, 102-104

Lamarck, Jean-Baptiste, 35
Lamarckism, 35, 40

language, xi, 27, 42, 51, 69, 73, 74, 75, 79, 80, 81, 82, 85, 86, 87, 90, 91, 92, 98, 110, 111
Large Hadron Collider, 46, 48, 54
leap of faith, 20
Leibniz, Gottfried Wilhelm, 14, 88, 112
Lemaitre, George, 54-55
leptons, 47
Lichtenstein, Aharon, 23
light years, 56-57. 64, 125, 128, 131
limitless, 84
linguistic, 83, 85, 93, see also "language"
literalism, biblical, 9, 67, 121-122
Lourdes, 101
Lucretius, 115
Luzzatto, R' Moshe Chaim, 94

Maimonides, xi, 11, 14, 23, 24, 90, 91, 92, 96, 127
Mars, 50, 117
Marx, Karl, 114
Mary's room, 75-76
materialism/ physicalism, 12, 53, 75, 123, 126, 137
materialistic atheism, 12
materialist/ physicalist, 18, 75, 76, 82, 131
Mathematical/extrapolative, 12, 15, 25, 60
Mendel, Gregor Johann, 36, 40
mental states, 73-74
metaphors, 111
metaphysical nihilism, 128
meta-science, x-xi, 4, 7-8, 34, 35, 131
methylation, 41, 41n29
Midianites, 86, 122
Milky Way, 3. 54, 57, 58
Miller, Stanley and Urey, Harold, 49-50
mind/body identity theory, 73

SUBJECT INDEX

miracles, 99-104
    embedded miracle, 101
    fortuitous miracle, 100
    fraudulent miracle, 100
    mistaken miracle, 100-101
    private miracles, 100-102
    public miracles, 102-104
Mishnah, 97, 122
Molecular genetics, 37-42, 53, 128
monotheistic, 11, 80, 81, 82, 83, 85, 94, 99. 104, 108, 113, 117, 118, 134
morality, 5, 6, 30, 106
    moral evil, 87, 89, 90
    moral virtue, 88, 89
Moses, 11, 22, 85, 95, 96-98, 122, 133
Muhammed, 99, 137
multiverse hypothesis, 14-15, 18, 26, 63-64, 131
myth formation, 102, 103-104, 113, 116-118, 134, 136

national memory, 102, 103
national revelation, 95, 124
naturalistic, 3, 4, 9, 10, 64, 109, 112, 115, 127
    natural disasters, 16
    natural evil, 87, 89, 90
    natural explanations, 45, 109
    natural selection, 16, 35, 53, 130
    natural theology, 18, 19, 23
Neanderthals, 70, 72
necessary existence, 14
negative atheism, 108
Negative theology, xi, 23, 90-93
neo-foundationalism, 21
neurons, 71, 72
neurosciences, 67, 72
neutrino, 47
neutron stars, 58
neutrons, 46, 47-48
new atheist, 30, 114
Newtonian physics, 54

noetic essence, 84
nones, 4-5
non-belief, x, 2, 4, 29, 54, 104, 107, 126, 131. 136, 138
non-disconfirmable, 90, 90n17
non-evidentialist, 108
    non-evidential faith, 18-23
    non-evidential theists, 134, 136
non-overlapping magisteria (NOMA), 6, 30
non-predicate theism, xi, 9, 10, 13, 79-93, 111
non-random, 51
nuclear fusion, 55-56, 61
nucleic acid sequence homology, 53
nucleosynthesis, 62

Occam's razor, 64, 64n49, 65, 131
Old Testament, 98, 121
omni- attributes, xi, 83, 85-87, 88, 108, 110, 111
    Omni-benevolence, xi, 83, 86, 87, 108, 110, 111
    Omnipotence, xi, 83, 86, 87, 108, 110, 111
    Omni-present, 83
    Omniscience, xi, 83, 85, 86, 87, 88, 93, 108, 110, 111, 119
    Omni-temporal, 83
Ontological, 5, 53, 81, 116, 124, 127, 134
    ontological argument, 13, 17-18
    ontological questions, 5, 53, 134
Oparin, Aleksandr, 49
    Oparin-Haldane hypothesis, 49
oral law, 22, 122
Oral Torah, 96, 97-99, 122-123
organic molecules, 33, 49, 50
organized religion, 106, 107, 113, 136
origin of life, 33, 49-50
Origin of Species, 31, 35, 48, 67
Origins of Religion, 106-107
Our lady of the overpass, 101

SUBJECT INDEX

Owen, Richard, 71

Paine, Thomas, 119, 121
Paleontology, 25, 52, 69, 71
Paley, William, 16, 44
Pardes, four sages, 12
pareidolia, 101
parenting drive, 53-54, 130
partnership between science and religion, x, 6, 7
Pascal, Blaise, 19-20
    Pascal's Wager, 19, 19n23
patternicity, 106
pedigrees, 51
peer-reviewed journals, 43
Penzias, Arno and Wilson, Robert, 55
personality, human, 71, 74, 80
Pew research, 4, 49
Photon, 47, 56
Physicalism/ materialism, 12, 53, 75, 123, 126, 137
    physicalist/ materialist, 18, 75, 76, 82, 131
pictorial imagery, 79, 80-81, 118
    pictorial theory of language, 80
Plantinga, Alvin, 17-18, 21, 88, 89, 112
pointless suffering, 87-88, 92, 119
Polarization, 29-30
polytheism, 117-118, 134
positive atheism, 108
prayer, 22, 77, 83, 84, 85, 86, 133
predicate, 9, 14, 17, 24, 80, 91, 92,
prime mover, 14
Principles of Faith, 96
promiscuous teleologists, 16
prophet, 11, 28, 83, 84, 85, 95-96, 99, 113, 133, 137
protons, 46, 47-48
Pseudo-Dionysius, 90
psychological, 2, 41, 106, 107, 118, 136

Ptolemy, 66
purpose, x, 4, 16-17, 18, 60, 63, 65, 93, 124, 127, 128, 133-134
    purposeful design, 16, 18

qualia, 76
quantum physics, 14, 45, 47, 59, 132
    quantum entanglement, 59
    quantum spin number, 47
    quantum tunneling, 132
quarks, 47, 55
quasars, 57
quasi-fideism, 21
Qur'an, 82, 99

radiometric dating, 52
randomness, 63, 65, 199
    non-random, 51
    random mutations, 16, 50, 51, 130
reality, metaphysical, xi, 3, 4, 5, 8, 10, 12, 15, 17, 21, 23, 24, 25, 28, 29, 34, 60 74, 80, 81, 82, 92, 105, 106, 118, 126, 128, 131, 135, 137, 138
rebellious son, 123
recombination, 56
red shift, 54, 56
Rees, Martin, 60
reformed epistemology, 21
refusal of medical treatment, 121
regress chain of causal relationships, 13-14
rejection of religion, 2, 29-30
rejection of science, 29-30
religious beliefs, origin, 106, 107, 110, 118
religious message, 9, 34-35, 99, 100, 104
repeatability, 25, 26, 27
reproducibility, 107
reproductive isolation, 51
resurrection, 99, 137

SUBJECT INDEX

Revelation, 8, 10, 22, 28, 31, 65, 77, 79-80, 82-84, 94-105
revelation, divine, 94-94, 104-105
revelation through miracles, 99-104
revelation, prophetic, 95-96
revelation, Torah, 96-99
reward and punishment robot, 12, 18, 113
ritual, 22, 106, 107
RNA-world, 33
rock strata, 52
Rowe, William L, 88
Russell, Bertrand, ix, 46n7, 114, 115, 117, 119, 124, 126, 128, 129,

Santa Claus, 109, 112-113
Schrodinger, Erwin, 59
Schroeder, Gerald, 32
science maturity, 138
   Science rejection, 29-30
   science-religion debate, x, 2, 6, 45, 46n7, 53, 63, 127, 128
   scientific concepts, 26, 27
   scientific facts, 26, 27
   scientific investigation, 7, 9, 18, 25-27, 76, 82, 123-124, 133
   scientific laws, 26, 27
   scientific method, 2, 9, 26, 28, 51, 52, 53, 107, 127, 129
   scientific papers, 34
   scientific theory, 27, 51
Scientism, xi, 5, 134
Scriptures, 9, 11, 22, 32, 67, 76, 83, 84, 8587, 92, 96, 113
Searle, John, 75
security, 82
selective pressure, 51, 77
self-referential, 20-21
Seneca, 114
sensate, 80, 81, 118
sensory, 7, 12, 21, 68, 79, 118
sensus divinitatus, 21

sexual drive, 53-54
Shermer, Michael, 106
Sigerist, Henry, 45
Sinai, 82, 95, 99, 102, 113, 124, 133, 137
singularity, 55
Sisyphus, 8n20, 34
   Sisyphean, xi, 34, 35, 60, 64, 125, 131
six numbers, 60-62
sleep, 76-77
Slipher, Vesto, 54
social benefits, 2, 107, 136
sociological, 2, 106, 107, 136
Soloveitchik, Joseph B, 23
Soul, 67, 73, 76-77, 77n35, 88-89, 112
   soul-making theodicy, 88-89
speculation in science, 26, 64, 70, 81, 90, 93
speed of light, 56-57, 64
Steinberg, Milton, 88
stellar dust, 62
Stewart, William H, 45
string theory, 60
strong force, 46, 47, 61
Swinburne, Richard, 17, 64

Talmud, 12, 68, 77, 97-99, 122-123, 133
teapot, 109, 117
technological benefits, 9, 27
teleological argument, 13, 16-17, 44-48, 54, 60, 130
Ten Commandments, 11, 95
Tertullian, 19
testimony to miracles, 100, 101-102
that's that, 46, 46n7, 106, 128, 129, 135
theism, xi, 2, 7, 9, 10, 13, 79-93, 111, 95
   theism evidential, 7, 134;
   theism, non-evidential, 108
theodicy, 87, 88-90

SUBJECT INDEX

theory in science, 27, 51
Tiktaalik, 52
timescale, 68
Torah, 83, 96-99, 103, 122-123, 133
    Oral Torah, 96-98, 122-123
    Written Torah, 96-98, 122-123
trait, 50, 51
transfection, 51, 51n21
translocation, 51, 51n21
truth statement, 3, 110, 112, 115, 116, 123
Turing, Alan, 75
    Turing test, 75

uncaused cause, 13-14
universe, 55-65, 66, 67, 72, 82, 93, 98, 110, 126n1, 127, 128-129, 130-133
    universe, complexity, 59-60
    universe, dimensions, 56-59
    universe, fine-tuning, 60-65
    universe, history, 55-56
    universe, regularity and harmony, 133

validation, 27, 28, 64, 95
Vienna Circle, 12, 12n4
Virgin Mary visions, 101

watch, human-manufactured, 16, 44
Watson, James and Crick, Francis, 37, 42
wave-particle, 59
weak anthropic, 63
weak force, 46, 47
weight of the human soul, 27n35
white dwarfs, 58
Winston, Robert, 126
Wittgenstein, Ludwig, 19, 20, 53, 79, 85, 98
world to come, 90
Written Torah, 96-98, 122-123

Yehuda HaNasi, 97
Yehudah HaLevi, 23, 102
youth, 4

Scripture Index

Genesis

1:3–26	84
1:26, 28	17
1:27	67
2:7	67, 76
1:28	78

Exodus

20:2, 3	11
33:18	11
33:20	11, 79
32:10	84
32:14	85
21:24	98
20:4	118

Leviticus

20:13	122

Numbers

31:1–18	122
12:6–8	96
15:32–34	122
31:17	86

Deuteronomy

5:6, 7	11
13:2, 3	99
34:10	96
12:21	98
21:18	123

1 Samuel

15:3	87, 122

Psalms

8:4–7	66
115:16	67
104	76

Ecclesiastes

3:10–11	18

Isaiah

55:6	138

Malachi

3:6	84

b Sanhedrin 32a, 34a	123
b Berachot 57b	77
b Berachot 33b	98
b Chagigah 14b	12
b Sanhedrin 108a	68
b Shabbat 127a	99

www.ingramcontent.com/pod-product-compliance
Lightning Source LLC
Chambersburg PA
CBHW050814160426
43192CB00010B/1761